STRATEGIC HR: DRIVING BOTTOM LINE RESULTS THROUGH YOUR PEOPLE

Printed in the United States of America

First Printing, 2020

ISBN 978-1-7342237-1-2
ISBN 978-1-7342237-0-5

www.edkrow.com

STRATEGIC HR: DRIVING BOTTOM LINE RESULTS THROUGH YOUR PEOPLE

BY ED KROW

This book is dedicated to the women in my life. To my wife Heather: your encouragement means the world. To my daughters Amanda, Emily, and Lea: you inspire me every day.

TABLE OF CONTENTS

"The HR function matters, but the HR profession does not."

—JOHNNY TAYLOR, SHRM CEO

INTRODUCTION

Human resources (HR) is, for the most part, irrelevant and has been for some time. Simply look at your favorite social media outlet and you'll find countless posts on the "why we hate HR" theme.

Years ago, an article was written that caused quite a stir in the human resources community. The article was entitled "Why We Hate HR," written by Keith Hammond in Fast Company Magazine.

Sure enough, there was quite a backlash in the HR community. Everyone was condemning what was in the article. But I remember reading it at the time and thinking, "It's a shame, but all of this is true."

Fast forward years later and I'm wondering, do we still hate HR? And if so, why? I took another look at Mr. Hammond's article and found that most of it, unfortunately, is still true.

I was recently at an event, a gathering of over a hundred HR people, on Valentine's Day. I was looking around at how this group presented themselves and I saw people wearing cute sweaters and fun ties with hearts on them. It's Valentine's Day, after all!

However, how do you take someone seriously when they're coming to talk to you about behavior change or disciplinary action when they have hearts on their tie or a Valentine's sticker on their sweater? Are other executives in the office dressed like this?

This is just one example, but many others come to mind. I recently participated in a meeting attended predominately by people new to the HR profession. During introductions, one person said that her background was in social work. She moved into HR to prove that "not all HR people are mean."

My initial thought was, "Well, that's good for you, but if you're bringing the social worker approach to the business world, then that means that you're not bringing a business approach."

The Real Challenge for HR

Therein lies the real challenge to HR. For all the progress HR has made since that article, one thing I still hear from company leaders is that executives look for ways to work around HR and not with HR. They see HR as the rock in the road. What's saddened me is that it's an earned viewpoint.

HR folks have traditionally not been business players. They're quick to say they don't get the respect they deserve. They're quick to demand a seat at the strategy table and yet have done nothing to break down those barriers to show they deserve to be at the table.

I realize I'm overgeneralizing here, and this editorial does not apply to all HR people. But the fact is, the HR function must change. It's not that everyone else needs to change and listen to HR. We must change as HR professionals and really learn what it means to become a true business leader.

That means truly understanding the needs of our business. Not just the people needs, but the business needs as well. Where is the business going? What is its strategic imperative? How do we as HR folks fit into that? We all know that HR should not simply be viewed as an overhead department, but what are we doing to impact that perception?

When I challenge HR folks, I often get the reply that "management doesn't want to hear that from me" or "my management team doesn't care about HR."

Two things pop into my head. One, that's a shame. Two, what have you done to cause that challenge?

I know that sounds pessimistic because I realize there are some business owners and some executives that don't value HR and no matter who is in the HR seat, they will not change their minds.

However, speaking from my experience, I just have to wonder: how many HR folks are really their own worst enemy?

More recently, I was in a meeting where the organization was evaluating their HR processes, because they wanted to put some new technology solutions in place. The CFO told me he thought we would find that some of their processes don't work. He didn't even finish his statement before HR jumped in and said: "No, you won't find that."

I looked at HR and thought, "Wow. Either we're really confident here, or we're hiding something."

We all have opportunities to learn. For HR to be that arrogant in a meeting and tell the CFO, "Yeah, we're perfect" is a shame and the death stare from the CFO confirmed what I suspected: he had no respect for the HR department.

This stems from two areas:

1. A lack of professionalism in the people serving in the HR function.
2. Most business executives view that HR is simply overhead.

Does this dynamic exist in your organization?

I've had way too many chats lately with folks who think anyone can do HR. They tell me that their CFO has a good handle on their HR processes. They tell me that their office manager handles HR. They tell me that their marketing person stays up to date on HR issues.

How is it possible for someone to effectively "have a handle" on HR when that's not their primary job responsibility?

I've been an HR professional for over 25 years, and there are days when I don't feel like I have a grip on all things HR because of the sheer speed at which things change!

For most organizations, HR is the biggest line item in their budget (typically about 30%). Yet we put someone with no professional HR background, whose main job responsibility is not HR, in charge of 30% of the budget because we think that anyone can do HR!

Think again.

HR is not simply overhead in your organization. That just doesn't make sense. But it's no wonder that's how we're viewed.

How HR is Viewed

Consider one of the more prominent HR characters in the media, Toby Flendersen of Dunder Mifflin. In an episode of The Office, manager Michael Scott asks Toby, "Why are you the way that you are? Honestly every time I try to do something fun or exciting you make it not that way."

When I think about the views of HR, it almost comes down to the idea that it's HR's role to make things "fun" in the office. I'm not sure I understand why HR is looked at as both the party planning committee and the fun police. No other department in business today has the responsibility for both making things "fun" and then policing that fun.

READ
Why your landscaper shouldn't be your electrician

So why is HR viewed as the center of all things "fun" in the workplace?

Recently, I was working with a $55M physician-owned medical practice and the HR team was not functioning at capacity. As part of my initial work, I was interviewing all the HR folks to get a sense of what was going on there.

I asked each one of them individually, "What is the goal of HR here?" All eight members said the same thing: "To make the people happy."

If we believe that people quit their supervisors and not their company, why is it HR's job to make people happy? Why are we not holding supervisors accountable for making their own people happy and satisfied in the work environment?

While a parody for our television, if we go back to poor Toby and the level of ineptness he shows, unfortunately, there's a level of truth in it because the average business professional I speak to has little respect for HR.

Whether they are at for-profit companies, academic institutions, or not-for-profit organizations, business leaders need HR professionals who are functionally knowledgeable and understand the business. As published in the book *The Rise of HR*, David Ulrich asserts that HR leaders will be viewed as strategic partners who can help solve real problems if they

- Use the business or entity strategy to drive HR activities.
- Understand the business and financial model.
- Know what drives success for the business. Does business success depend on innovation,

capital utilization, customer connectivity, service excellence?

- Understand the business metrics (such as profit, margin, Return on Investment (ROI), free cash flow productivity) and what drives them. For example, if your company uses Total Shareholder Return (TSR) as a key performance metric, the HR leader should know the specific metrics that drive TSR.
- Determine the skills and capabilities needed to deliver the business strategies.
- Identify the top talent and match them to business-critical roles.
- Determine the organizational risks that could jeopardize the company's business success.
- Design organizations that deliver outstanding business results.

What HR Should Be Doing

The sole purpose of HR must be on affecting the business.

Just like every other department that gets paid to bring solutions to business challenges, HR must move away from being a "people advocate." To be clear, I am not advocating that we move back to the ways of the sweatshop. However, it is imperative that HR better understand how the people of the business help the business succeed, not the other way around.

HR should not be the "corporate police," the "compliance department," the "party planning function," or serve as the "Chief Paperwork Officer." These functions are administrative in nature and can be handled by any non-HR person.

READ
The Big Problem With HR

I want HR to embrace change. To let go of the status quo, of rules, of procedures. I want HR to rise up from mediocrity, to no longer be the bastion of the "this is how we do things" mentality.

I want HR professionals to be strategic thinkers and well-rounded business professionals. I want the HR function to be staffed by the best and brightest minds in business and to once and for all squash the mindset of business leaders who believe "anyone can do HR."

I want HR to move beyond developing rules and procedures and focus instead on developing processes and strategies. To stop worrying only about the legal ramifications of decisions and worry about the business ramifications of decisions, too.

If you're reading this and wondering, "Okay, but how do we make that happen?" That's what this book will explore.

Because I know this to be true: HR can be easy. We make it hard.

Low-level thinking, failing to understand what makes our business successful, and an inability to articulate the worth of the HR function creates an environment of failure.

Successful HR can be boiled down to developing an HR strategic plan that supports the company's strategic plan and boosts the organizational culture. Based on that HR strategic plan, develop your plans for learning and development, compensation and benefits, performance management, and work-life fit.

Getting those items right will lead to the attraction of quality talent and the retention and motivation of the talent we already have. This, in turn, leads to engaged, productive employees who will drive business results.

If HR would focus solely on business success, we would have the coveted "seat at the table." We would be respected as business partners. Our contribution would be easily measured and no longer seen as overhead, but a necessary investment for growth and success.

Finally, I know there will be detractors to what I have written here, including many in the HR profession. While everyone is entitled to their opinion, the loudest complainers about my statements will be those folks simply scared by what I've outlined here. Too scared to change, too scared to admit that the old ways don't work and haven't for years. Unwilling to face the new business realities and unwilling to realize that they are part of the problem.

READ
Creating a Strategic HR Function

That's why the title of this book is *Strategic HR: Driving Bottom Line Results Through Your People*. We are going to break the mold and rebuild it! This book is for any executive who recognizes that business can only succeed through its people and is looking for the roadmap to get there.

We'll explore what I believe are the key activities we must do as executives to ensure we are managing our human resources functions effectively and that they are delivering the business results we require.

"Connect the dots between individual roles and the goals of the organization. When people see that connection, they get a lot of energy out of work. They feel the importance, dignity, and meaning in their job."

—KEN BLANCHARD, AUTHOR, *ONE MINUTE MANAGER*

BUILDING EMPLOYEE ALIGNMENT

1

For HR to contribute to the results of the business, it must first understand the strategic imperatives of the organization it serves. HR must go beyond being a function into being a piece of the business.

For instance, for HR to solve a business's problems, it must first understand why those problems exist. It must be able to identify those hurdles and bring solutions to the executive team. This requires HR to think outside of its function.

I was recently chatting with the CEO of a manufacturing organization and his number one complaint about HR is that HR fails to help him figure out what his next strategic moves are with people management. He told me that in all his experience as an executive, he has found HR to be nothing but bureaucracy police more interested in handing out "speeding tickets" than bringing solutions to the table.

He said, "I have a business to run and I need HR to be part of that business, not just a function dedicated to building its own empire."

Those are some pretty powerful words and the shame of it is that you will hear that theme from CEOs throughout the book. HR has routinely not done a good enough job becoming the strategic player it needs to be. We'll look at why throughout the book, but a key reason for this is that HR typically fails to look outside its own function.

HR doesn't exist to be the party planning committee or make employees happy. It exists to bring success to the organization. Organizational success is what will drive employee success.

By staying focused on the bigger picture, we then get to impact folks at an individual level. For HR to be that strategic team player, it must understand the business strategy of the organization. There are typically three accepted business strategies. In this chapter, we'll look at each one and explore why a business may go down that road. More importantly, we'll discuss what HR must do regarding that strategy.

Business Strategy: Customer Intimacy

A business whose strategy revolves around customer intimacy drives revenues through its relationship with its customers. It's the age-old "we put our customers first and therefore they want to work with us" mentality.

Businesses with high-level customer service like Nordstrom, Starbucks, and luxury car dealers belong in this category. Some folks have argued that Southwest belongs here. Any business that has fiercely loyal customers would fall into this category, regardless of the product or service the business is offering.

Often, customers will pay more to deal with these businesses because of the relationship they have with the product or service. HR must ask itself: if we're operating in a customer intimacy environment, what types of employees do we have to hire that will follow that mantra?

A classic example of a customer intimacy business strategy is Disney. People pay huge money to vacation there every year, and some families go year after year to have that experience. Disney is well-known for its commitment to a customer's quality of experience and the level of customer service training it puts into its people.

The question for HR becomes, what types of people are we looking for that will maintain that level of intimacy with our customers? What types of benefits, rewards, and training and development opportunities are we going to put in place to allow our people to thrive in a customer intimacy environment?

Later in the book, we'll talk about ways to identify these things in detail but for now, these are the questions HR must ask itself regarding customer intimacy.

Strongly focusing on customer service, it makes complete sense to recruit people with a strong commitment to helping others. Perhaps all your interviewing and recruitment messaging is based on coming to our organization because we help make others' dreams a reality–we make our customers the happiest there are. In this way, HR's employment and recruiting brand must marry closely to the product or service brand of the organization.

Business strategy: Product or Service Leadership

An organization that focuses on product or service leadership is focused on putting the best possible product or service that money can buy on the market. Customers will pay more because they're the best.

An example that comes to mind is Apple. Apple always has the latest and greatest electronics that money can buy. Let's be honest–their phones don't do much more than any other phone, yet their customers are fiercely loyal to them because of the quality of their product.

Think about high-end hospitality chains like the Waldorf Astoria. The level of quality service that's put out by an organization like that makes people spend more on their hotel than another hotel.

When we think about that top-notch product, we must think about what types of people we will recruit to provide it.

For a company like Apple, we need engineers to build that product and we need geniuses at the Genius Bar who know the ins, outs, bells, and whistles of everything on the floor. The HR message will be different from their employees because the typical employee will ask why they're not focused on the customer. HR must be prepared with a message that says, we are focused on the customer through providing the highest level of product or service on the market. We'll come back to crafting that message later on in this book.

If HR is functioning in a business focused on product or service leadership, it will look very different than an organization with a customer intimacy model.

Business strategy: Operational Excellence

The final key business strategy is operational excellence. This organization drives its value to its customers through how it runs its own business. Some organizations that use this strategy are UPS, FedEx, and Wal-Mart. A company like Wal-Mart has an excellent logistics and distribution system that drives down its cost to its customers.

The challenge for the HR function in this environment is that the people who drive those operational efficiencies often never see the customer. They're working in warehouses, trucks, and distribution centers. Their attention to detail will drive how well the product or service is delivered to the customer, so again the HR messaging in recruiting, hiring, and development must be very different. How do we keep the employees focused on the end game—a customer buying a widget at Wal-Mart or receiving a package from UPS—when they never actually see the end game?

Again, if HR is functioning in an operational excellence model, communications with employees will differ significantly from the two previous models discussed.

HR's Role in the Business Strategy

It's important for HR to understand which of these three business models they're operating in. To be fair, all businesses have a toe in all three strategies. But one is usually the driving factor. I guarantee that whether it's formally noted in the strategic plan or not, the C-Suite knows what it's trying to do and where it's trying to go regarding these three strategies. They've already determined how they want to drive value to their customers.

HR's role in driving value is in helping to figure out what that role is and more important, developing the HR function to support the business's goal. I was recently working with an organization that was very customer focused. They're a healthcare organization, so obviously, their strategy is product or service excellence. People go to their practice because they're the best at what they do—at fixing bad joints and broken bones, and rehabbing ortho-skeletal problems.

The challenge for HR in this organization was that it didn't identify itself with that goal. The organizations' goal was service leadership, but the recruiting message didn't pair up with the organizational message. The owners (who were all doctors) were concerned that if the employment brand didn't soon pair up, it would affect their marketing brand.

Here, we can see a small example of how critical it is that HR understands the business strategy and develops its own strategy around that. Once we identify the business strategy, everything else should come out of that.

Why Does Business Strategy Matter?

For HR, the two most important things are our HR strategy and our workplace culture. Once we identify the business strategy and work on the HR strategy to support that, we're at a point at which we can affect the company culture.

I routinely get asked about the main drivers of company culture. There are many, mainly because of leadership and the management style within the organization. Many organizations whose culture suffers because of leadership and management suffer because they have not identified key strategic imperatives.

WATCH
How to Communicate Your Strategic Plan

Given their management team, HR should understand the skills and tools they need to succeed inside the business strategy. When we fail to give our leadership team those skills, our culture deteriorates. If HR doesn't have its strategy wrapped tightly into the business strategy, if they're not pulling the right levers to create the culture that will support that business strategy, we have a huge problem. The business is a thriving organism like the human body, and everything is connected.

Often, we might feel pain in the body in one spot. When we go to the doctor, she may find that the pain is actually coming from an entirely different part of the body. Where you're experiencing pain is simply where the pain is manifesting.

We see this same exact scenario inside business. Unfortunately, too many business leaders play whack-a-mole with their business problems. They think that if they just replace that one leader or spend more money on that employee appreciation event or bring in that well-known speaker for their leadership program, their business will get "fixed."

But most problems go much deeper than that. It comes back to whether or not we have identified our strategy and linked every piece of what we do back to that strategy. When our company gets sick, it's usually because we have ignored something related to HR processes. The only way our company can stay healthy is if the people in the organization are driving business results. It's only on very rare occasions that the business gets sick because of external issues. The economy can determine that but little else outside of the business controls business success like the humans we have helping us inside it.

So, if we believe that, then it's critical that the HR strategy considers the key things that make employees willing to work hard and commit to the organization's mission. It all starts with communication: how we communicate to our people about why the plan is what it is.

What's the message we're sending to our people?

That message is critical, and HR must step in and be the driver.

Another company I worked with was dealing with employees complaining about a lack of communication from the HR function. It was an 800-person organization spread out over nine facilities all geographically close to one another.

I found that HR was communicating, but all of it was through email. Some emails were 3-4 pages long of information!

When I asked HR why they were communicating like that, their response was that they want to be sure everyone gets all the information they need. That's great, but the problem is that no one wants to read a 3- or 4-page email, so people just weren't reading it! Much of the information didn't apply to everyone in the organization, and HR did absolutely no tailoring so one department could focus on what mattered to them while another department received a different message.

Communication is an imperative skill that HR functions must develop to be a strategic player in organizations. It's not just about the ease of getting messages out, crafting the email and hitting send. It's about the quality of the content and clarity about what's being communicated. When we look at the World at Work Model later in this book (Chapter 3), we will see that the HR strategy enables us to focus on the five key areas that are imperative for HR to be masters of in the organization, one of them being communication.

Working with client focus groups can help improve employee opinion results.

Communication issues kept coming up as a problem in a large international organization that makes a lot of products found in our homes. You'd think in a large, well-known organization like that, they would have figured out communication. As we met and I heard different ways this organization was communicating, I believed that perhaps they were over-communicating with their people. Perhaps they were sending too many messages.

One of the biggest problems we found was so simple to correct you wonder how an organization of this size could make this mistake. At one meeting, a gentleman said, "I'd like us to take a field trip. Let's go down to the cafeteria." In the cafeteria, there was a large 20-foot-long bulletin board. He said, "Ed, take a look at all that's up there."

I did and there was lots of good stuff. There was information about company activities, about benefits, even some of the company's financials. He said, "Look closer." So, I did and then it hit me. One of the things the organization did was have regular town hall meetings. The plant manager would get up and talk about the state of the company including key metrics like on-time delivery.

All of that is well and good. The problem is, all the employees at this facility from sales to R&D to drivers were at this meeting and her message wasn't tailored for any individual group. It was very broad.

But that wasn't their biggest mistake. The company was the American division of a German-owned entity. When I looked on the board and sat in the town hall meeting, every financial metric being reported on was reported in Euros.

That might seem trivial. If someone tells you your business profit is a million euros, you know that's a good thing. But the problem is obvious. As an American, unless you really follow financial markets, you probably don't know today's exchange rate. What do a million euros mean in American dollars? We understand that we're up, but how much?

Businesses do this all the time in their own way. They may use lingo that new employees don't understand or use lingo prevalent in one department and not another. When we craft these messages about why we have the strategy we have and report on those things, it's critical that our people understand the message and where it's coming from.

How Communication Impacts Employees

HR must develop a total rewards strategy as part of its strategic plan to impact the culture and business results. It must design a compensation and incentive program centered on rewarding the behaviors that support our business strategy and drive business results. It must design a benefits package that's not only fiscally responsible for the organization but one supportive of their recruiting efforts to get the best and brightest talent available and again to reward employees for giving us their time and effort.

We must design a performance management system with goals aligned to the departmental goals that flow up to the organization's goals. Gone are the days where everyone in the organization has the exact same performance review. We must get much savvier than that and we'll talk about that in this book. HR must develop a learning, development, and opportunities program aimed at enhancing the skills of its people to support business goals and drive results. Employees must see the connection between learning on the job, the skills they were hired to exhibit, and how those skills drive the business forward.

It's imperative we consider work-life issues in this. We know the demographics of the workforce. What might different folks in the organization be looking for in work-life fit at this point in their careers? If we can stir that total rewards mix up properly within the organization, we are not only going to have satisfied and engaged people, we will have a solid employment brand in the marketplace with people knocking on our door to come work for us. It's impossible under those circumstances to not hit our business goals and objectives because the business machine will be firing on all cylinders.

Ultimately, everything starts with the business strategy, which drives HR strategy and organizational culture. From there, how we communicate with our people will be the determining factor of our success.

We'll talk more about HR strategy in the chapters to come. But when we have a disconnect between the business strategy and HR, we can't possibly get business results. We're off message. In the medical group I was working with, every HR person there thought their goal was to make people happy. That's not the goal of any HR function anywhere.

It's a nice outcome of some of the strategic things we do and to be sure, a satisfied and engaged workforce will be more productive and likely derive more job satisfaction. But to focus solely on making employees happy is not being a strategic player. It's not helping the C-suite make the business decisions it needs to make.

I once had an HR director complain about having meetings with the C-suite and owners. She said, "Ed, our turnover isn't the greatest. I gave them the numbers and they don't give a *^%."

My response to the HR director was–I'm not surprised they don't care about the turnover percentage! What they care about and what you're not telling them is what that turnover percent is doing to their business. You need to tell them in dollars what turnover is costing them. You must tell them in dollars what it's chipping away at in the bottom line, how it's affecting their ability to service their customers. That's what the ownership group and C-suite need to hear. They don't care about the percent, so stop telling them!

WATCH
Communicating Your Stategic Plan

The sad thing is this isn't a one-off scenario. I hear this routinely from the C-suite when I talk to them—that HR folks come into meetings, spout off percentages, and leave. The very same HR people who do this complain to me that they don't have a seat at those meetings and aren't asked to contribute.

I respond, "It's because you're not contributing anything of value. You're reporting on numbers. The C-suite wants to know why the numbers are what they are and what to do to fix them. Wrapped around all of that is what the financial impact is on the business if it's not fixed."

Business executives: you deserve better! Another CEO told me he specifically hired an HR Director who came with a marketing background because she knew how to communicate effectively. Show me an HR function with excellent communication skills, and I'll show you and HR function operating at peak performance and affecting the business.

Next, we'll look at how to develop a strategic plan for HR that focuses on driving business results.

"I am convinced that nothing we do is more important than hiring and developing people. At the end of the day, you bet on people, no strategies."

—LAWRENCE BOSSIDY,
FORMER CEO, ALLIED SIGNAL

CHARTING HR'S COURSE IN YOUR ORGANIZATION

2

In the previous chapter, we talked about the importance of first selecting and communicating out your strategic plan. Let's now take a deep dive into how to put together an HR strategic plan.

A study was done in 2015 at the University of Michigan looking at what impact HR competency has on business performance. They did the study repeatedly over the course of about 16 years, and they found this: if HR really wants to impact the business, they must show strategic contribution.

But here's the problem: I don't know that a single HR person I've ever spoken to has actually put together a formal HR strategic plan.

WATCH
How to Get Results from Your HR Function

They may have pieces of it—I often hear that they have a "great recruiting plan" in place—but that's not enough. HR folks must think about all the other areas that go into HR. What are the key things that really allow you to drive strategic contribution to your business? There are six key areas HR must address in its strategic plan to be sure it links with the company's overall strategic plan.

Market Trends

The question to ask HR is: what do you need to know about market trends? One thing we may need to understand is what the market looks like for the product or service we're offering so that if we must hire more people or expand areas, we can plan for those things. There might be emerging areas of business or new areas of growth for the organization.

From a strategic perspective, we might want to be working with customers to see what the labor needs might be, where we have gaps in our organization, and how we need to develop capacity within our organization.

Maybe we want to get into new lines of business or want to get into a new geographic market. What must HR consider about those things? What are the impacts on HR if we decide to do those strategic initiatives? Let's say we're diversifying the business, bringing in new products and services. Do we have the resources we need in-house in talent? Do we need more people or just different types of people? We're going to have to analyze our talent and decide if we need to hire or train from within.

We also must consider the economy and the role it plays in decisions. When we think about the economy and our business response to the current economy, can we project out what that will do to us five, ten years down the road?

Are our talent needs going to be the same or different in that time frame? The scary thing with talent management is training is a big part of that. When the economy is good, we put a lot of time, effort, and money into training programs. The problem is that when the economy turns bad, one of the first line items to get cut is training. When we need people operating at their best, we pull one of the very resources from them that can help them do that: ongoing training!

As business leaders, we must plan for inevitable downturns in the economy. We must make sure we are still investing in our people so they can be highly productive for us when money gets tight in the business, so we're prepared to weather that storm.

Key Business Metrics

Often, I'll hear an HR person say that turnover is a key business metric (KBM). The problem is, it may be a KBM for HR but it's likely not a KBM for the rest of the organization. Nobody cares what percent of turnover we have. What management cares about is what it's costing in money walking out the door–the cost to replace that person, the cost to hire. Can we monetize what turnover is doing to us? That's the metric that actually matters.

What we also care about with turnover is who is leaving. If all my poor performers are leaving, I'll take high turnover! If the people leaving are high performers, even a small percentage of turnover is bad.

The problem with HR is that they're usually not measuring the right things.

I have a client in the long-term care business. They rave about the fact that their one facility, which is typically a hard department to staff with a lot of turnover, is at 3% turnover. I looked at that facility to figure out why they had such a low number.

The company has been around for 50 years and has grown tremendously. This particular facility was one of their earliest ones. They don't have some of the original employees after being in business for 50 years, but some people have been there for twenty, thirty years. Here's the problem: what they're finding is that younger people are turning over. Younger folks don't want to do the jobs they have. Their 3% turnover rate is masking that it's a handful of positions turning over again and again because they've got a very senior workforce.

That senior workforce is now in their late 50's, early 60's. They're going to retire in the next 5 years. I can guarantee that without attention to why younger generations don't want to do their jobs, they will go from 3% turnover to 80% turnover in the blink of an eye because the stable piece of that workforce will be gone! But all this time, HR is patting itself on the back for that 3% rate because they failed to take a deeper dive into that metric.

Another client had a horrible turnover rate on one shift only. The more we dug, we finally figured out that it was a racial problem. They can't keep African Americans on that shift.

There are obvious discriminatory concerns there, there was no turnover with any other race category. It had been going on for a while, and we needed to take a deeper dive to look beyond the percentage of turnover and say, "Now that we know African Americans are leaving, we have to figure out why." These are the types of strategic analyses HR has to be doing for the business. These are the things management must hear about.

Regarding the shift turnover scenario above, all that management kept hearing for years was, "We have very little turnover." When I questioned them further, they said it had been going on for a while now. I said, "Who's looked into it? Do you understand the situation you're putting yourself in with one race turning over faster than everyone else combined?" I wondered what HR had been doing all this time, why they weren't looking at this seriously and sharing this concern with management.

Performance, both individual-level and department-level, is a key business metric. But the bigger question to ask ourselves is whether the performance management tools and processes we have in place are effective and how we know they're effective. What are we measuring with our tools?

If we are not measuring specific goals and objectives at the individual level and department level that pair up with the goals and objectives of the organization, our performance management system is failing.

Are we worried more about making sure performance appraisals are done and reporting back to management that we're 98% effective in getting them done on time? Or are we taking a dive in to see that 98% of our people are hitting our goals? That's a key business metric, not how many performance appraisals we've done on time!

Again, HR gets in its own way by measuring the wrong things. The other thing to look at is where these goals are coming from.

A friend is in banking. He switched to a new bank and was given a new set of goals he thought were reasonable and that he could hit during the course of a year. By May, he had hit his goals. The obvious problem is that maybe the goals weren't aggressive enough. He landed a monster deal that put him over the top, but one deal should not allow a salesperson to ace their goals for the year!

We have to be smarter about how we set goals with people and how that rolls up to the department level through the rest of the organization.

We often hear that employee engagement is a key business metric. The challenge with that is how we quantify having engaged employees. Perhaps we can do an engagement survey, but we must take a deeper dive into what drives engagement. I know many organizations that do employee engagement surveys and do nothing with the results of those surveys.

So, let's look at things like absenteeism, productivity, and turnover. Those metrics together can give us a feel for whether we have an engaged workforce. The bottom line is when we set performance goals for someone, they must be able to own that performance goal and impact it. I recall many years ago when I was at UPS, a KBM in that world was delivering a package from point A to point B in the shortest time. Note this was prior to the scanning capabilities and technology they have today.

The facility in which I handled HR processed about 50,000 packages per day. On average, we received 6 packages that didn't belong there each day. That's not a bad ratio unless that's your box sitting there, right? Here's the problem: we, in that receiving facility, got dinged for those boxes showing up. It went against us on our performance review. But that doesn't make sense. We couldn't impact what was showing up in our facility. All we could do was train our people on how to handle it. So, our whole management team took goose eggs on a metric we couldn't control. Talk about demoralizing! With technology today, it's different, but 20 years ago we didn't have that. We can't punish people for things they can't control and have no responsibility for.

I always ask businesses; do you have metrics like that? Do you have metrics in place that people can't control? It could be something that's at the whim of nature, perhaps if you're a seasonal outdoor organization or a lumber salesperson (who hopes for hurricanes so you can sell lumber for the rebuilding!). Those metrics don't guarantee us the sustained performance we need to grow our businesses.

The bottom line is if you have goals on people's performance reviews they can't control, you're killing motivation. That will kill your strategic plan because people won't be working towards the organization's objectives!

Training might be a key metric, but unfortunately, most organizations view training as an event. The employee attends, we check a box, and we're 100% compliant. If training is a key business metric for us, we should be measuring what behaviors changed and were sustained because of the training that took place.

If I don't go to the annual harassment training, what really happens? If I'm not harassing anyone and no one is harassing me, nothing happens yet we get all get worked up if someone doesn't attend. I'm not saying that's not important, I'm saying that if someone has been going to a repetitive training for the last 10 years, should we be looking at delivering that training in a different way?

I handled an industrial accident a while back where a maintenance mechanic failed to lock out his equipment and lost the tip of a finger. He has been to every lockout tag-out training he was required to attend for the previous 10 years. Yet he still chose not to apply his training because he was at the far end of the building and knew it would take longer to shut off the equipment and return. So, he decided to make the fix and someone at the other end of the building started the machine.

Some would argue this was a motivation deficiency, not a training deficiency but it certainly is a training deficiency! The behavior he was taught didn't stick. That's a problem. The training didn't stick, so the behavior didn't change and that's how we should measure training. Are we seeing changes in behavior relative to the training we put out there? It's not about how many people went to what. It comes down to effectiveness.

Another thing to look at for training is ROI. Say it costs $15,000 to put a training program together. What did you get out of it? Let's say this isn't about checking a box for compliance purposes but bringing in leadership development programs for our people. What are you getting in return for that $15,000 investment? Is our management team able to use the new skills to better lead and motivate people? Is turnover decreasing and productivity increasing because of that? We must measure these things regarding training.

If we want to be more strategic leaders, we must be measuring whether the training was effective and whether the behavior stuck following training, not checking boxes.

Another key business metric is retention. I look at retention and turnover differently. With turnover, we want to analyze who's going out the back door. Retention is more proactive. We're looking at who we should be retaining.

Who are your power players, your most impactful people? Have you identified your high performers? Are the right people in the right seats on the bus?

These are the metrics we should be measuring! I don't care how great a widget you have if the people working for you are horrible at selling it or horrible at installing it.

Thinking about retention means thinking about who is critical to the organization. We focus on high profile positions, but maybe it's that part-time store clerk in retail or the home installation repair person we need to focus on retaining because our customers like to know they have the same person showing up at their home to conduct preventative maintenance on their HVAC system.

I'll often ask folks who the most important people in the organization are. I get all types of different responses, but I come out of UPS and when I ask who the most important people at UPS are, most people will say the drivers. I don't disagree–the drivers are certainly critical.

But the drivers can only deliver what's on the vehicle. The people who determine whether the drivers get the right boxes are typically a bunch of part-time employees working during the night. There are two to three times as many of those people as there are drivers! Those people never see the customer, but they have the most impact on whether the box shows up in once piece, not damaged and on time. Drivers don't control those two things.

I challenge readers to ask, "What jobs do we have that are critical and not customer-facing? How are we retaining those people?" These are key business metrics to think about. Who do we need to retain, and do they understand their connection to the customer even if they never see them?

Now let's look at financial analysis.

Financial Analysis

Often HR will say that one of their financial metrics is wages or percent of overtime or cost of benefits. I don't disagree–we definitely need to keep an eye on those. But are they the true metrics we should worry about?

When it comes to wages, we will probably pay what the market is paying so we can get good people. With overtime, maybe we can manage that but perhaps folks are working a lot of overtime because we have a lot of work coming in. And we all know that our ability to control the costs of medical benefits is limited.

With the HR department and its financial metrics, I say they must look at where they're spending their money in those areas. They need to look at the entire total rewards package.

The financial analysis that matters is: are we getting the most bang for every buck of our investment in our people? The employment relationship is very simple. We put together a package of working conditions, pay, and benefits that will attract the talent we want. That talent comes in, shakes our hand, and says yes, I will give you 100% of my effort on this job in exchange for the pay, benefits package, and working conditions you have described.

That's the employment relationship! When organizations struggle with turnover or recruiting or motivation, my first question is: where are you spending your money?

Do you have the right mix of those total rewards? Even more important, do people understand the value of those total rewards? For instance, do you have a company holiday party and a significant portion of employees don't attend? Or those that do complain about the cost to bring a spouse or significant other? Does a significant portion of your staff have to work the party or picnic to make it happen so it's not a fun day for them? Why are we spending a lot of money on events that aren't getting us any tangible return?

I believe in looking at every single thing we do and determining whether it is driving what we want it to drive.

I have a client who does one Employee Appreciation Day per month. It could be as simple as hot chocolate on a cold winter day, cold sodas on a hot summer day, or donuts and coffee.

It's a healthcare organization and most of the employee appreciation days revolve around free food. The employees complain that there's a wellness initiative at the company, but the free food is always pizza, donuts, soft pretzels, something like that. This makes little sense! It must be part of our financial analysis because they're spending a lot of money on their health and wellness initiative and employee appreciation initiative, and those two initiatives don't connect. There's no cohesiveness of message!

It sounds terribly simple but when was the last time we actually looked at all the things we spend money on relative to our employees? Let's determine whether they actually want these things! Many organizations spend money giving everyone a mug or t-shirt with the company logo (and it's not a bad thing to do). But many people don't want to wear and use things with the company logo on their private time! It's not because they're not proud of where they work, it's just a preference and a fashion decision.

I once heard of an organization who changed its logo. They did a big reveal at an all-hands meeting held at a local conference center. For the second half of the day, they left the center and their families were invited to come to a local amusement park.

One thing they handed out to everyone to show off the new logo were temporary tattoos. Temporary tattoos were great when you were a kid, but how many adults want to slap on a temporary tattoo of the company logo, even if it's just for a day? That's just silly!

Sure, the temporary tattoos didn't cost a lot of money, but this is an employee relations decision here. It was completely wasted time, effort, and money.

Meanwhile, I've got another client that gives employees a gift certificate for a birthday cake every year for their birthdays. And 99% of the gift certificates get used every year. They're good for a couple of months, you don't have to use them right away, and you can custom order the cake you want with whatever decorations, style, flavors you enjoy. It's simple and people love it!

Sometimes we overcomplicate the things we're doing for investing in our people. I'll discuss this later in the book, but one of the biggest things we can do is simply ask our people what they want.

So often, we change benefit packages because we're trying to save our people money. That's certainly admirable. But I have a client who has changed their plan and the providers associated with it each of the last four years straight. Management says we held costs! That's great! But they're asking people every year to adapt to a new plan. Medications weren't covered are now covered and vice versa. Pay scales are different for procedures than previously. That's way too much disruption for the savings they were experiencing.

Rather than just looking at the benefits package in a bubble, look at the implications. Give your employees a choice! Say we can lower costs, but we must switch, which will result in X, Y, Z. Or, we can stay with our existing plan and it will cost a little more, but your coverage stays the same. We can get feedback from our people, so we know whether we're wisely using our financial resources.

I had one organization tell me they cover 100% of their employee's medical costs. I said, "Wow, that's incredible."

The client said, "Yeah, but I don't think they appreciate it," and gave me some examples of why. I said, "Then you need to stop doing that."

He looked at me with wide eyes and said, "But this is a huge benefit!" My response?

"It is. But your people are telling you they don't want it, that they don't see the value in it!"

I recall a while back working with a professional services firm with pretty good starting pay. It wasn't quite at the level of their competition, but they offered free company smartphones to everyone and that made up the difference. The problem was, it wasn't affecting recruitment. We asked candidates about it, and they told us they don't care about the free phones, they already have a phone! They really wanted to link in with their own phone and be paid the market rate.

Management kept saying, "They don't understand the value!"

My response was, "Who cares? Their perception is that they want more in their paycheck on Friday that they can make their own decisions about money with. Stop giving away company phones!"

We're our own worst enemy when we try to force these issues thinking we know what's best for people. But believe me when I say that if we give people what they want (within reason), that's money well spent! They will have a higher perception of the value of what we've given them if it's something they actually want.

I think when we look at financial analysis, compensation must be a huge piece. We must regularly know what we're doing in the marketplace against our competition. When I speak to clients about this, they often think their only competition comes from their industry. But really, their competition for talent is anyone hiring the types of people they're hiring.

While that sounds simple, most organizations don't view their talent competition in that way! If they're a food processor, they think they're competing with other food processors.

But if someone can operate a food processing machine, there are probably other types of machines they can operate as well. Therefore, anyone hiring machine operators is likely competition for their talent! We must be willing to take the blinders off for assessing the money we're spending with our talent pool. Who are we comparing ourselves to? We should be comparing ourselves to other like-sized organizations and organizations with similar geographies as well as our own industry.

Another financial metric worth considering is the HR-staff ratio. I often hear that the HR staff is determined by the number of people in the organization. That's one way to look at it, but let's also look at what adding HR staff will do to the bottom line of the organization.

I once had a large client with 100 open positions and over a 55-day time to fill in those 100 positions. We figured out what those open positions were costing them, and our cost-benefit analysis showed this organization could save significant money by adding another recruiter. So, we did that. Time to fill went down to 45 days but more important, open positions dropped to 30 within 3 months.

Rather than looking at our HR staffing model as solely a number of employees to the number of HR staff ratio, sometimes we need to look at it in a cost-benefit analysis. If we will bring in a $50,000 recruiter, how much money are they going to contribute to the bottom line in filling vacancies quickly, paying less overtime, and creating a workforce that's less stressed and less prone to making mistakes? Here, which was a healthcare environment, it's critical to not make mistakes. The staff was suffering from burnout and we had to fix the problem fast. It was a no brainer to spend the money on another HR person to save many times over the cost of their compensation and benefits.

What it comes down to is this: we must know how our company makes its money. If we go back to the previous chapter on different types of business strategies, how does your organization truly make its money?

You might be surprised if you ask that question. One of my clients is a regional airport authority. People think they make their money on passengers coming in to take flights. But actually, the bulk of their revenue comes from the tenants of the airport–the airlines, restaurants and stores, and air cargo facilities within the airport. They're actually much more of a real estate manager than a typical "airline facility." Once you understand that, now HR knows the skill sets it needs to hire to be in that environment.

From an HR perspective, when's the last time your HR staff spent time out on the floor with your operations managers? On a ride-along with a salesperson? Listening in on customer service phone calls?

If you can't remember the last time HR did that for you, then there's no way they have a good grasp on how your company truly makes its money which means they cannot financially affect the organization the way they're currently managing it.

The next thing we have to look at with HR strategic planning are environmental changes.

Environmental Changes

Environmental changes can be anything from changing laws that impact our business to political changes to the natural environment outside changing to technology changes. Environmental changes are really anything happening outside our four walls impacting how we do business and our ability to do business the way we want to do it.

One thing I think is critical in knowing about your environment is knowing what customers say about the organization. We often spend so much time focusing on our employees (and that's good to an extent) but how are we engaging our customers? And what does that have to do with developing a strategic plan for the HR function?

Why should HR care what our customers think? Isn't that just a sales and marketing responsibility?

HR has to know where the customer stands because it directly correlates with our employees. If the employees we are hiring and training can't make the perfect widget, mow the perfect lawn, care for the patient properly, whatever you do, you will have unhappy customers.

When you have unhappy customers, it always comes back to something related to our employees. It could be related to motivation, training, poor hiring, performance management, any number of things- and it can be hard sometimes to get that sort of feedback. If you're in the hospitality business with tools like Yelp to see what customers are saying, it may be easier.

But regardless of industry, customer-facing employees and sales folks know exactly what customers think about us. We must be willing to talk to those folks to discover what's going on in the eyes of our customers.

Often when speaking on this topic, I'll ask the question what's it all about? The majority of people will say it's about the people making the widgets and mowing the lawns. I say, "No, it's more than that. It's about our ability to sell and market the products and services that we are engaging our people to make or serve."

When we think about our environment and the pressures we get externally, often pressure may come from our competitors. If we want to have an effective HR function, that HR function must understand what our competitors are doing that's affecting our ability to do business. I'd suggest attempting to do a SWOT analysis on your competitors.

The Competition

What do we perceive as their strengths, weaknesses, opportunities, and threats? Who are they?

Here's where often folks get mixed up about who their competitors are. A landscaping business may perceive their competition as other landscapers. If you're in hospitality, you may think of other hotels or restaurants. For healthcare, it's typically other medical practitioners. These are direct competitors, yes.

But the HR function must understand that a competitor is anyone with whom we are competing for talent. You might not mow lawns but perhaps the talent of the landscaper down the road is the same talent you need in your restaurant or on your assembly line. The traits of the workers may be similar, and so we must open our minds to who our competitors really are.

Often the best talent is already employed. So, if we're going to find the best talent, we must lure them away from where they're currently employed. To get the traits we've identified as key, we want to be willing to look outside of our industry.

Often when I'm chatting with HR, they'll tell me something like, "I don't have to worry about that, I only have 5% turnover and the industry average is 10%."

I say, "So what? You're the only company within 100 miles of here who does what you do. Who cares about the industry average? Tell me what your turnover is compared to other organizations in your geographic area that are hiring the same kinds of people you are hiring." That's a more critical piece of the environment we need to be concerned about. We want to know what they're paying, the benefits they have, the work environment they offer, and are their people happier than ours? Find that out!

When I say that, folks will often say they don't know how. Aren't you members of trade associations and professional associations? Don't be afraid to go, network, ask these questions to find out what's going on in the work atmosphere outside of your four walls.

When we go to these types of events and network, what we're really trying to do is figure out how we get the right mix of people in our organization. What does that look like for us? How do we put the right mix of rewards on the table for them so we don't lose them?

Maybe technology impacts your business heavily. We must look at how we're using technology inside our organization to benefit our people.

For instance, I was working with an organization that implemented a new Human Resources Information System. It was one of the top products on the market and it came with a hefty price tag. This organization was implementing the new system in pieces, which was really smart because it had tremendous capabilities.

The problem is, they never trained their people to properly use the technology. Therefore, folks feared using it and didn't use it to its full capability! Often, it was actually hindering some of their efforts. For example, the recruiting function wasn't keeping up with the status of applicants inside the tracking mechanism and that resulted in emails being sent to people inquiring about whether they were still interested in employment when they had been working there for over six months. That's a terrible slap in the face to someone!

Technology is always part of our environment, and it's constantly changing. HR must figure out how to harness and use it to better serve the people in their organization.

Another piece of technology that many organizations have is assessment. They'll use personality-type assessments to gauge the new hires coming in the door, to screen applicants, to better develop in-house folks, and more.

I'm amazed at the number of companies I deal with that have salespeople they've never put through assess-

WATCH
Stop Moving Your Targets

ment and when they finally do, they find these are great people, but they can't close a deal. They can talk, smile, and market services in the best possible light and often customers love these people because they bring things like pizza and donuts. But they can't close a deal! And that's a problem. Those folks might make good account managers because they keep customers happy, but if they can't close a deal then they're not a salesperson.

If we want to pull these six areas together and think about the impact they have on the ability of HR to drive results in an organization, we can see that if the HR function doesn't properly analyze each of these six areas, they cannot possibly put together a strategic plan that drives results.

However, there is a dark side! We can put all this work in, develop a solid plan, and it can still fail! How? By failing to watch out for these five things:

Communication breakdown. Typically, if I'm in a room talking about strategic planning with people who aren't executives, I'll ask the group if they know if their firm has a strategic plan. Usually about half raise their hands.

Then, I ask them to keep their hands up if they've actually seen it. About 80% of the hands drop. Can you see the issue here? We know executives go on a retreat to a swanky resort and say they're developing a strategic plan. They come back with a nice binder and no one ever sees it. But that makes little sense.

The same is true for HR plans. If we put an HR strategic plan together and don't share it outside the HR function, don't talk to our peer leaders, and don't talk to the executive team about how the strategic plan will support the business, that plan won't work. Remember: we can't operate on an island as HR.

Our ability to effectively communicate key components of the plan and what they will do to support each business function and the organization is critical to meeting our key objectives.

Lack of leadership. Often, HR is an understaffed department. Many are departments of one...and that doesn't bode well for someone who struggles with delegation. Someone smarter than me said this, but I'm a big believer that "the only way to get things done as a leader is to get them done through other people." We must get rid of what grandma told us about doing it yourself if you want it done right. That approach doesn't work in today's business environment.

The failure of leadership is the failure of an HR person to delegate some responsibility for the execution of the HR plan to others in the organization who may actually lie outside of HR.

For a lot of professional firms like accounting and engineering firms, recruiting is housed outside of HR. They send engineers out to talk to engineering students and accountants out to talk to accounting students. Other areas HR often fails to delegate to include employee retention and engagement. Those belong on the front line too, and we're setting the plan up for failure if we take no leadership role in giving folks the authority to help HR manage the plan.

There's no plan behind the idea. I've reviewed many plans for HR in various organizations and they're full of lofty ideals like "we want to be the best" and "we want our customers to love us." That's fine, but those are just nice high-level ideas. A strategic plan must be more. It must have the meat in there that tells us how we will get customers to love us and how we will get to be the best at what we do.

If we don't have specific goals and objectives laid out, and if there are no accountabilities lined up for meeting objectives with a specific timeline, we can't expect to meet our strategic imperatives.

This is more unique to HR than many other departments because while everything we do can be and should be measured, we fall back into things like "we want to increase our employee engagement."

But what does that mean? How will we measure it? How will we know when we've met that goal?

At times, I feel like HR doesn't measure things like they need to but, on the other hand, sometimes they put measures on things unnecessarily. Take turnover for example. What happens if we want to reduce turnover to 5%? That's a noble idea, but some turnover is good. We want fresh ideas coming in! What are we doing to decrease turnover and does it really serve the organization? Are we increasing pay too much, and not holding people accountable when we should be?

The key is to understand what you're measuring and why.

Passive management. For fans of The Office, I call this the Michael Scott syndrome. Passive management means assuming things run themselves once you start them. Obviously, that's not what really happens.

This comes back to my point about leadership: though you have mastered the leadership piece and delegated responsibility for parts of the plan out of HR, you still must remain the leader and hold folks accountable. There need to be mechanisms in place for periodic check-ins and check-ups on the strategic plan. Too many organizations dust off their plan once a year and ask, "where are we?"

LISTEN
Ed's Strategy Podcast

If you have a three-year plan, that binder should be beat up and falling apart from being so well-used.

Our strategic plan should be talked about in HR department meetings. It should be talked about as part of any other strategic imperative. It should become part of all our decision making.

Lack of motivation and personal ownership. Whether it's your HR team or folks you've delegated portions of your plan to, team members must understand how getting behind those goals will support the company and their own personal career goals.

Often, I see strategic planning focused solely on where the company is headed. That's one important area where the HR plan must be different. The HR plan must include the component of what you'll do for your people to help them meet their goals.

The obvious challenge is that you must know what their goals are, so you can write a plan to incorporate getting them where they want to go (which helps the company get where it wants to go, too). These are not silos. They must go hand in hand.

Honestly, this is where a lot of HR folks miss the boat. They get too worried about being the advocate for the employee and forget that if we set up a good HR strategic plan that's going to support the organization and we weave in the components to support our people, we're helping to make everyone better.

I think ultimately, it's important to remember that HR is a business function. That's the strategic imperative in HR, and it's no different than finance or sales or IT. HR has a business imperative to support the organization, and I can guarantee that other functions have strategic plans in place as well. IT will know what kind of technology is coming down the pipeline to help support the organization and will have plans in place for it. Sales always has a sales strategy.

So, I'm always a little dumbfounded when HR has no formal HR strategic plan, especially when asking "what's our most important asset?" Most executives will say, "Our people."

So why don't we have a strategic plan for managing the people function of our organization?

I invite you to ask yourself: given what you know about your current strategy, what must you do from an HR planning perspective? If you don't know your company's current strategy, what are you going to do to find that out so you can put together an effective HR strategic plan?

"However beautiful the strategy, you should occasionally look at the results"
—SIR WINSTON CHURCHILL

THE IMPACT OF HR STRATEGY

3

Often, I'll ask the audience at a conference how many have a succession plan for leadership in their organization.

Typically, 90% of hands will go up. Most organizations have a transition plan for the C-Suite. But when I ask how many have a plan for their mid-level managers, typically only about a third of the hands go up.

That's a huge problem because mid-level management really gets things done for us. They're the rubber bands, the link between our people and the C-Suite. Ultimately, they're responsible for making the six items we talked about in the previous chapter actually happen.

In a tight labor market where turnover isn't where you want it to be, you must think about a succession plan! Wouldn't you want to identify your high-performing employees and put a plan in place to retain them? What happens if that critical employee wins the lottery or gets ill? What would we do? What are the positions like that, that keep us up at night? That's a huge piece of the HR strategic plan that many organizations miss.

We'll talk more about succession planning in a later chapter. It's critical that you have a succession plan not just for top management, but for the nuts and bolts of the organization—your front-line managers, your mid-level managers.

We'll talk too about organizational and cultural changes in the organization, and all of these things are reflected in our strategic plan, but we must have a plan! I once had a business owner say, "We don't really have a culture around here."

I chuckled and said, "What? Of course, you do. You just don't know what it is."

That's bad! That's like saying that your family has no traditions. We all do, whether they're conscious and intentional or not.

With the HR strategic plan, we must think about the cultural impact and what we're trying to do inside the organization.

If you want to be an employer of choice, what does that actually mean to you in today's business environment? What is your employment brand? I'm working with a client now who tells me he thinks the culture is fine in his organization. The problem is, it's not what his employees actually want.

Sure, to a certain extent his culture is fine for him. He's in a highly creative industry that attracts young Gen-Z folks. They're asking for simple things like a Keurig for flavored coffee and he's bucking. He thinks it's silly.

I say, "What's that really going to cost? A couple of hundred dollars?" That's a no brainer! He may not think it adds value, but his people are telling him it would. Who cares if he thinks it's ridiculous? What are your people saying to you?

Sometimes as business owners and executives we get in our own way. We must think about what our culture is right now and what it should be. If there's a gap there, what are we going to put in place to get it to change?

This all comes back to our strategic plan. We don't just come in and say, "We're going to change the culture today! We're going to buy pizza for everyone and have dress-down Friday and now we have a new culture."

That's silliness. Culture change must be planned, managed, and be a part of our overall strategic plan.

So, let's look at the World at Work diagram. It encapsulates what HR needs to be concerned about in one simple picture. Everything starts with the business strategy, as we discussed. That seeps into the HR strategy and that impacts the organizational culture.

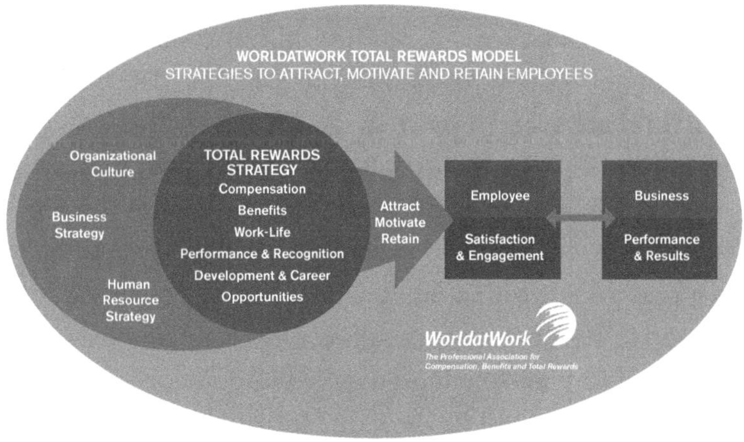

Those things wrap around everything else we do for our people. Way too many organizations have a business strategy but no defined HR strategy. They have a culture that has just evolved but either isn't one they want or one that will sustain the business. And they come to me because they're struggling with their total rewards strategy.

They tell me they're not able to attract, motivate, and retain the best people. People are dissatisfied and disengaged, and it's resulting in them not getting the level of performance and business results they need.

I share this diagram with them to show that they're missing two key components. You must work at your culture. We can't possibly have satisfied and engaged employees who get business results if we have no strategy to figure out who those people are, what they want, and how we will implement it.

HR can be quite easy.

When you think about the employment relationship, it really is nothing more than us shaking hands with a candidate, saying, “We’ll pay you X amount of dollars and give you these benefits in exchange for you giving us 100% of your effort and achieving these results.” They say, “Yes, I accept those terms.” Later things fall apart, and we wonder why!

Why it falls apart is because from day one in the organization, the environment is changing a little. By month six, year one, year five–the entire workplace has changed. We created this exchange of results for this level of money and benefits, but that exchange may now be out of whack and we haven’t revisited it. We don’t look at how the culture is evolving, for better or for worse, and how that may be affecting the strategy we have around HR.

Ultimately, this is when we start to lose our people’s engagement. When they start to become dissatisfied, it’s nearly impossible for the business to achieve the performance and results we need it to. One overarching thing in all of this is work-life fit.

I work with a wonderful business coach who preaches that we need to work in our “joy and genius zone.” That’s a powerful insight when it comes to work-life fit. We should know where our people’s joy and genius zones are and allow them to get into that zone.

What if their genius zone is at 4 in the morning or 9 at night? Not between 10 am and 2 pm? Why not let them work at the time and place that’s good for them? They’ll be happier, and we will get more results from them.

This is a mindset shift but it’s coming and it’s coming fast. We now have an entire workforce we call digital nomads. They work where they want, when they want, they’re producing great results and guess what? A huge part of the latter part of millennials and a big part of the Gen-Z folks entering the workforce have this mindset. So, we need to harness it.

Your Homework

I want to wrap this section up with a few thoughts, you might even call homework. Think about where your company is currently. Do you have a strategic plan? Maybe you don't and that's okay. You probably have an idea of where your organization is headed and that's enough to get started. Maybe you have a formal strategic plan and you're thinking, "Ed, I can't incorporate all this into my strategic plan—we're already in year three of a four-year plan."

My response is yes, you can. I bet you have no strategic plan for HR. You now have the basics to start that, but what's going to come next is tying it into the overall strategy of the business.

You can't wait until you're formulating your new business strategic plan to do an HR strategic plan. Given what you know about your current business strategy, what do you need from the HR function to achieve that strategy?

One client has 5% of their positions open. It doesn't seem like a lot until you recognize that 5% is 40 positions. Part of their business strategy is opening another facility across town, and they'll be doing that in 9 months. That's going to generate 70 new positions.

Now that 5% vacancy rate looms large because they must hire for those 40 positions and in 9 months, they must come up with 70 more employees. These are skilled positions, and they have no plan in place to make that happen.

We have to take a step back and look at each of the six items we've discussed and make them part of our HR strategic plan. I would even go out on a limb and say those six items can and should be part of our overall business strategic plan as well.

But think about what we need to be concerned with in each of those six items. How are those items affecting our business today? Maybe even more important, how will they impact our business in another year or three or five?

Because after all, that's where the true benefit of a strategic plan is—being a bit of a prognosticator, saying not only where we want to be three, four, five years from now but where is the outside world going to be and how will that impact us?

WATCH
Is Remote Work a Business Necessity

You're not going to knock this out in an hour or two. You're going to need to spend quality time in thought and talking to other members of the executive team. Building an HR strategic plan should take several months. Anything less and you haven't uncovered all of the potential challenges you might face and identified all the ideas to overcome them.

What Are We REALLY Paying Our People to Do?

One challenge that comes to mind is remote work. This is a huge concern today as more employees want to work remotely, yet employers are still resistant to make this happen. Often when I speak with business owners about this, they tell me, "Well, if they're not here I won't know they're working."

My typical response is, "If they're behind a closed door in their office how do you know they're working?"

If you hired someone you couldn't trust to work for you and get results for you, why did you hire them? We must break the mindset that work has to be done in a particular way at particular hours in a particular place.

These are industrial revolution concepts. While certainly if you run a manufacturing floor, people must be there to run machines at certain times of day. That's understandable. But I bet there are scores of employees in your workforce who could easily work remotely for you.

Remember: we are paying and rewarding people for results, not for the hours they put in.

I'd like to share a story of a mechanic who had retired from his organization where they fixed locomotives. There was a locomotive giving the rail company fits, and no one could figure it out. The CEO called the retired mechanic and asked him to please come in and take a look.

The man agreed and spent all day tinkering around, looking at things, tapping here and there. Finally, at the end of the day, he took a hammer to this one spot on the locomotive and whacked it hard two times. The problem was fixed, and the locomotive was back in shape again.

The CEO was thrilled and told the mechanic to send him the bill. The man sends a bill for $10k, and the CEO says, "You were here for one day and you tapped twice! Explain this bill."

The mechanic said, "Absolutely." He itemized the bill into 2 sections: tapping on the machine to fix the problem cost $2. Knowing where to tap cost $9,998.

This is what we pay people for. We pay them for their results, not the time it takes to get those results. If we want a high performing organization, we need an HR strategy that harnesses the power that our people have to drive results for us.

Google famously gives its people 20% of their time to work on whatever they want to work on. Some of Google's best products have come out of that time! Think about that: for one full day a week, Google says "Go, do whatever you want." It must be business-related but go do whatever you like! Be creative! How many of us would be willing to allow our people that level of freedom?

WATCH
ROI vs COI

But that comes back to the culture we're trying to build in our organization and the culture supported by the business and HR strategies.

This mindset can often be applied to working with outside vendors as well. When we're looking for vendors to help support our organization, perhaps it's an outside consultant with a specific area of expertise we need for a temporary period, remember that we're bringing that person in for their expertise and not their time.

I will tell you the consultant who comes in and says they'll work for a set fee per hour will not drive the same results as the vendor who comes in and says yes, I will achieve these results and here's the fee for driving these results.

Too many business owners want to know what an "hourly rate" is when they should be focused on the ROI they will get from bringing the expert in. The railway executive was so concerned about the $10,000 invoice when what he should have been worried about was what it's costing to have this locomotive sitting there out of commission for weeks on end. Had he thought about it in that regard, he would have easily signed off on the $10,000 check!

I began this chapter with some initial thoughts on succession planning as a key piece in our HR strategy. Let's look at what it takes to pull an effective succession plan together that will support our business objectives.

"I am more interested in people than I am in how businesses work."

—PETER DRUCKER, MANAGEMENT THEORIST

SUCCESSION PLANNING: THE BUSINESS CASE

4

With the training and development of our people, one of the most strategic things we can do not only for our people but for our business is to create a succession plan.

Unfortunately, succession planning is often the most overlooked piece of the learning and development puzzle. This is because most businesses think succession planning is one of these things:

1. Ensuring that we have an owner or executive to take over in event of the passing or retirement of the current owner or executive.
2. How to move the entity from one generation to another…from our lawyer friends.
3. Moving dollars from one generation to another… thanks to our friends in public accounting.

Don't get me wrong, certainly, these are all valid succession planning concerns and business owners would be wise to consult business attorneys and CPAs for advice on those fronts. However, from a strategic HR perspective, if all we do is succession planning for the top job, we have no way to ensure the true viability of the business which typically lies in our middle management function.

In this section, I will talk about the importance of succession planning for middle management and how to develop mid-level bench strength in the organization.

If we will develop the future leaders of the organization, we must start with our ability to develop the talent we already have. I hear a lot about the "talent shortage" experienced in today's economy. When I talk to executives about that, they'll tell me they can't find and recruit people with the skills they need.

My question to them is typically, "Okay, that's a valid concern. What are you doing to bridge the skills gap with your current workforce? Can you develop your current workforce to eliminate the skill shortage you're seeing?"

Unfortunately, more often than not, the executives I speak to say, "We've never thought about that."

The common misconception is that we can only recruit for skills, we can't train up some of those same skills. In certain areas, that may be true. But through a solid learning and development program, we can build the skills of our people and have the bench strength we need to keep the business viable.

The Challenge to Learning & Development

The biggest challenge to overcome when looking at our skill levels and specifically succession planning is when we have plenty of money in the budget, we don't mind investing in the training and development of our people. But when we're in a tough economy or the business takes a downturn, often the first line item to get cut is training and development.

This is counterintuitive. When the economy gets tight and business takes a downturn, we really need our people at their absolute best. So just when we need them at their absolute best, we take away one of the tools we have for getting them to their best, which is training and development opportunities.

I see training and development as an investment. Yes, we invest in our people and there's no guarantee that if we do, they'll stay. That's the biggest objection I hear from executives.

However, I believe in this saying often attributed to Richard Branson: "Train your people well enough that

READ
How to Grow Your Future Leaders

they can leave but treat them well enough that they'll stay."

There's a lot of wisdom in that. People leave organizations for a number of reasons. We want to make it tough for them to leave because of the environment we've created in our organization.

One thing we must think about with training and development and specifically succession planning is that to be effective, we must be willing to invest in all levels of our people. We want to specifically focus on how we develop our mid-level management team. We're not only developing folks that can move into mid-level management functions, but we're developing those already there to assume positions of greater responsibility.

The business case for succession planning

Let's talk about the business case for succession planning. What's in it for us?

Recently, the Corporate Leadership Council conducted a survey. They asked organizations to predict within the next 3-5 years if they will see an increase in leadership vacancies.

72% of the companies in the survey responded "yes." The scary part of that was that of those companies that said yes, 76% of them said they were "less than confident in their ability to staff those positions."

If we only apply succession planning to the C-suite, we are making a grave competitive mistake. I'd like to use a definition of succession planning that's the best I've seen, from Dr. William Rothwell, Professor of Education, Penn State University.

He defines succession planning in this way: "It is a deliberate and systematic effort by an organization to ensure leadership continuity in key positions, retain and develop intellectual and knowledge capital for the future, and encourage individual advancement."

I find that definition powerful on several fronts, and I'd like to break down each piece of it.

He talks about succession planning being deliberate and systematic. Later in the book, we'll talk about how learning and development need to be treated as a process and not as an event. That's what Dr. Rothwell is saying here–that we must have a mechanism in place to ensure these things are a part of the systems of our business. That learning and development (and specifically succession planning) are ingrained in everything we do.

The other important point he makes is stressing key positions. I'd ask readers to ask themselves, "What are my key positions? The important thing here is if you're honest with yourself, some of those key positions may not be the lofty titled positions. We must open our minds up to decide what positions are really mission-critical to our organization.

I would take Dr. Rothwell's definition one step further and ask, what people in your organization are mission-critical?

Those two things are very important distinctions to make. We may have key people not in key positions, and we may have key positions not filled with the right people. We'll discuss this in greater detail later.

The second half of the definition really tells us why we need to be doing this. In today's economy, which so many people acknowledge is a true knowledge economy,

Are Millennials a Problem?

Today's workforce not only is more mobile in its career path but most sociologists agree that the millennial generation and now Gen-Z will have multiple career changes. Yes, career changes where they are reeducating themselves and going down a completely different path from where they started. They'll do this multiple times throughout their adult work life.

Most people see this as an impediment to the business succeeding. I say, let's harness that!

I'm currently succession planning with an airport with a millennial-aged employee who had a great attitude but was failing in her job. They weren't sure what to do with her. They knew how valuable her outlook and attitude were, and she was trying hard, but it just wasn't working out. During the succession planning project, I had a discussion with her department lead. We talked about her strengths and what she brought to the table, and we realized the strengths she had weren't needed in the job she was in–and the strengths required were ones she didn't possess.

So, in my discussions with her department head, I said we have two choices here. We can train her up to get her the skills she needs to succeed, or can we find her another job in the organization that needs her skill set.

At this point, the department head laughed. She had assumed the second choice would be "or we fire her." But I am too much of a believer in the importance of attitude and outlook, and finding someone with that mix is so key to our business that I want to hold on to that. Firing this woman who otherwise was trying hard every day, was the cowardly way out.

We found a position we thought she could do well in, discussed it with her (she knew she wasn't succeeding in her current role), and she decided she wanted to give the new role a try.

Fast forward nine months later and she's killing it in her new role. She's now in the succession plan and undergoing the training needed to one day perhaps be the department head of her new department.

I use this story to illustrate that we have talent right under our noses in many cases. But we must harness it. Here's someone that management was ready to give up on, but we had only to take a step back to think a little differently.

I often hear about these "millennial kids." The sad thing about that view is that the eldest millennials are in their mid to late 30s now! They're not kids by any stretch of the definition. They have homes and families. They're 10-15 years into their careers. These are well-established professionals.

One good business friend, who is a millennial said, "I'm tired of being called a little kid. I'm in my mid-30s, I am a homeowner, my husband and I are planning to have kids. I'm a big girl now!" We had a good laugh over that and yet that's so true. My point is, let's not use the millennial generation and their views on work as an excuse to not invest in our workforce. Millennials, just like every other generation, can be fiercely loyal if their needs are being met. One of their big needs in the workplace is professional development and the opportunity for advancement.

There are tremendous benefits to the organization that has an effective succession planning process. We become much more proactive and able to anticipate workforce gaps. We're no longer reacting when someone hands in a two-week notice of resignation or when our long-term employee says, "I think I'm ready to retire now" and we didn't see it coming.

If we have a solid succession planning process, we're able to identify the employees that are high potential and help them plan out their careers. Most important of all, we're able to align our people strategy and our business strategy. If we can meet those three requirements, then we're talking about creating the level of leadership capacity that's going to drive sustainable business results for your organization.

I recently spoke with a CEO who had lost a very valuable employee, and they were sad to see this individual go. The employee left and was successful in her new position. But they kept in touch and after three years, she came back to the organization and said, "I'd like you to keep me in mind for a role with your organization again."

Because she left under good terms and kept in touch, eventually a position opened, and they brought her back. The CEO sat down with this mid-level management person and asked her to tell him about what had transpired. She said, "I felt like I needed to leave to grow a bit." She had been with the organization for all 10 years of her career at that point, had some advancement, and felt she needed to move on to have other experiences. When she came back, she told the CEO that she wanted to come back to the organization for the culture. She said, "Yes, I learned some things at the other organization. But I love it here."

As business executives, we forget that sometimes we must let our folks go for them to realize how good they have it. But we also must keep the door open and not resent that they left. A good succession plan, as we'll see, recognizes that maybe our key people will need to leave the organization to address part of their professional development. But if they're treated well and offered everything they need, they'll come back to us more valuable than ever.

What Does a Best-in-Class Organization Look Like?

When I think about the companies that are not best-in-class with succession planning, those companies are 100% reactive to what is going on around them. They are shocked when someone turns in a resignation. They're surprised when an employee takes early retirement. Then they run around saying, "What are we going to do?!"

I dealt with a situation where a gentleman had been telling his employer he was ready for another step, some additional responsibility. He had been hitting his goals and was ready. This was an extremely large corporation with plenty of opportunities to be had, so that wasn't the issue.

The issue was this organization's view on how one moved through the ranks. At every stop, this person attained the business results expected of him–sometimes even better. He took on special projects and was seen as the go-to person for specific knowledge in the organization. He had expressed interest to his department head about being ready for new challenges. An opening came up that he wasn't particularly interested in but would have been qualified for and it would have been a promotion. It went to another person and he was okay with it.

Here's where the story goes south. The department head, thinking she's doing the right thing, sat down with him to talk about why he didn't get the position. He said, "It's okay, I understand. The lady who got it is perfect for that role. I applaud her for getting the promotion."

Rather than stop there, the department manager said, "I want you to know you were in the discussion, but we realized we couldn't let you both go. Because you're so valuable, we need to keep you here."

This same department manager was completely surprised a month later when he turned in his resignation.

I ask you to think about why we should be surprised when a highly talented, highly motivated individual asking for additional responsibilities and is ready for them, leaves when we hold them back for our own personal gain. We cannot possibly expect that this person is going to remain committed to us. In fact, when this man turned in his resignation the exact words of the department head were, "I don't know what I'm going to do now that you're leaving."

READ
People
Empowering
Leadership

Today's business imperative above everything else is to hold on to our high potential employees. This organization's bureaucracy hindered that.

If we contrast that with an organization that is best-in-class with talent management, they view learning and development as an ongoing process. They recognize that the greater good has to be served, sometimes at the sacrifice of the lower level of good.

Here, the department manager trying to hold on to the person rather than letting him be all he could be for the organization not only lost him out of the department but lost him from the organization. Best-in-class companies are inclusive and develop large pools of talent because they recognize that some folks in the process will fall out. They may fall out through leaving the organization, failing to rise to the occasion as they're given more opportunities, or perhaps because of life changes that may inhibit their desire to move up.

The key is that management must own the process. This isn't something we can delegate down. It's critical that senior management make the determination "this is important to us." You'll find when I go through the steps to succession planning that it's quite simple to implement a learning and development culture that results in an effective succession plan. But we also must make it transparent.

Folks must know where they stand in the process and why. This scares a lot of executives. When we go back to the situation I just mentioned, the man went so far as to tell his department manager he would take a relocation with the organization if it meant he could fulfill his next level of career goals.

He was transparent with the organization about where he wanted to go and what he was hoping to do regarding his career. But the transparency wasn't two-way. That was a culture challenge for this organization.

I implore executives to be transparent about their succession planning process. I'll go into detail about the reasons this works and why we don't need to be as overly concerned about some of the problems with being transparent as to how we're developing our people and why.

In the next chapter, I'll uncover the method of developing a succession plan that works for the company AND its employees.

"Succession planning doesn't start with people. It starts with the requirements of the position."

—DAVE ULRICH, PROFESSOR, ROSS SCHOOL OF BUSINESS, UNIVERSITY OF MICHIGAN

SUCCESSION PLANNING: GETTING STARTED

5

Best in class succession planning organizations use a proactive approach to planning for upcoming leadership vacancies. They know that succession planning is an ongoing process, not an event where once the plan is done, it sits on a shelf. The succession plan becomes a living, breathing part of their team and individual performance management and development processes.

The larger the organization, the more important it is that this process is inclusive and that you develop a large pool of management and leadership talent. This is the point at which an organization must decide how transparent their succession plan will be. I believe it must be quite transparent in that the people in the plan must know they're in the plan, know what they're in the plan for, and be fully bought into and supportive of their role in the plan. For example, if Sue is the heir apparent in the finance function, she should know and be willing to assume that responsibility.

On the Job Development

For succession planning to be proactive and ongoing, management must own the process. They must own their individual AND their people's development responsibilities. One way we can do this is to emphasize on-the-job development. Too often, organizations believe that sending people off to a seminar, having them take a college course, or doing some classroom training is enough to get an individual ready to assume a position of greater responsibility. The reality is development doesn't happen in class; it happens on the job. We must look for ways to create progressive assignments for folks to make that happen.

I'm a great example of that. During my time at UPS, I reached a point where I was ready for additional responsibility. My manager at the time was also being groomed for additional responsibility. For him to grow, he had to delegate some of his work to free up time to pursue his needed professional development goals. He and I reviewed some things on his plate and he selected a few projects he thought I would be interested in. I agreed I was interested. His delegating helped me grow by taking on some of his work, and it allowed him to offload some of his projects to work with the division-level manager on assuming some of those responsibilities.

WATCH
Why People Quit

Often managers say they don't have time to develop their people. My view is, as managers, developing people is our prime responsibility. Our most important responsibility is to develop those around us and make them successful.

It Can Start with Delegation

When we think about designing these assignments, we really must make sure that we scope out the assignment and the expectations for the employee. The operative word here is delegating to the employee, not dumping work on them.

Delegation implies it's a well thought out project with pit stops along the way to check in. It means we're there to work with the employee when they start to struggle with the new assignment—because remember this is a stretching assignment for them. For it to be a true development assignment, we must be there for them as check-ins throughout the process.

Probably just as important is that the development must be individual to each employee. One-size-fits-all doesn't work for succession planning. If we're grooming someone for a position, we must tailor the learning to that specific position and person. What do they know now? What must they know to assume the position and what's the best way to fill the gap?

Part of that comes back to providing ongoing coaching and feedback.

Here's the problem: if we don't successfully develop our people prior to them assuming new positions. Studies show that 40% of all newly promoted managers fail within 18 months simply because they weren't able to build a strong team or strong relationships with individuals on their team.

The Peter Principle

Think about your organization. Do you promote someone, shake their hand, and say, "Go get 'em, tiger?" Or have you developed them into that position, so you know they will be successful when they assume that role?

If we don't develop our people, we fall prey to the Peter Principle. The Peter Principle is nothing more than promoting people to their own level of incompetence.

I see this happen quite regularly. Think about the assembly person on the line who is a great assembly person. We say because they're a great assembly person, we'll make them the supervisor of the assembly line. That's a completely different skill set to manage the line and the people on it!

Let's assume they shift into that role and can do it successfully. We then say, "Gee, they made such a great supervisor, let's make them the manager of the assembly department."

But again, taking that leap requires a new skill set–managing other supervisors. The Peter principle says that if we only promote based on current successes, sooner or later we'll promote someone outside of their skill set. They'll get overwhelmed and we'll wonder why they're failing.

The only way to avoid the Peter principle is through a strong organizational development program focused on individual success.

One of the best ways to do that comes back to on-the-job development. Rather than simply relying on a standard curriculum, we must develop managers and future leaders through challenging and diverse experiences.

This might mean they need some experience outside of the department in which we're developing them. Perhaps someone we're grooming to be an operations manager might need a rotation through finance, HR, or sales to get a good understanding of how the other side lives. We must be careful with this type of training as well because as they're in these assignments, they still must be held accountable for their goals and development. Failure to do that is just checking a box saying, "They spent time here so they're good to go."

The message here is we must be sure as an organization we understand and nurture each employee's unique talents and potential. Then we must evaluate our talent pool and identify both leadership gaps and suitable candidates.

Should We Tell People They are in the Plan?

I recall working with an organization a while back that had identified their future Executive Director. She was currently the Director of Marketing and on paper was very qualified for the Executive Director position. She had all the experience, the relationships with the staff, and the business savvy required.

The problem was, she didn't want it. When I sat down to talk with her while working on the organization's succession plan, she said, "I'm flattered, and I love this organization, but I love marketing. The next step for my career is going to be with a larger organization that has a bigger marketing function for me to manage."

The moral here is if we succession plan to the exclusion of talking with the people in the succession plan, we're in for some surprises when the time comes to elevate someone into a new role.

For identifying candidates, another key piece is that the executive team must be highly involved through group discussions and review sessions about where the talent is in the organization. Who are the key knowledge holders? Who are the current high performers and who are the high potentials?

The danger zone in this part of the process is we can get into too many corporate politics. Favoritism has no place in this part of the discussion. The executive team must be completely bought into the fact that it's not about who they like on individual teams but who is the best for the organization to continue to help the business grow and meet its strategic goals.

Once we identify those folks, it's time to open a dialogue with them. This is where we talk with the employee about their successes, their strengths, what they believe their needs are, and their aspirations. This step is critical. Remember, the person we really want may not want that role, or they may not be ready for it right now.

A lot of work-life issues will come into play through this process. I've talked with many young parents who tell me they don't want the promotion right now because they'll have to travel more. They're happy with their jobs now and want to be able to get to the ball game and be home with their families. In five or six years they may be ready to take it on, but not now.

As we're succession planning and talking with folks, we must keep those work-life issues in mind.

I recently had a situation where a high-level manager opted out of the succession plan. She was nominated for a C-suite position in the organization, but she was now the primary caregiver for her elderly mother. The new position would have come with travel, longer hours, and there would be no one at home in the evenings to care for her elderly mother. Work-life issues aren't just with young parents, those caring for elderly parents have similar concerns.

A Coaching Culture

If the succession plan will work, we need a culture shift in the organization towards a coaching culture where development is ongoing, not something you do once a year in a performance review. For many organizations, this is a big shift.

I'm currently working with an organization on firming up its compensation and performance management system. One of the cool things they already have in place is quarterly one-on-ones with their people. It's not a formal sit-down performance review but a one-on-one catch up. The employee and their manager sit down, review their current goals and development, and talk about what's needed for the upcoming quarter. These talks are usually only about 20-30 minutes, but both management and employees find it critical to the success of the company.

That organization has a coaching culture.

If you have folks who are great managers but not great coaches, look outside your organization! If there are gaps in their knowledge base, let's get them some leadership coaching so they can coach future leaders. No matter how we slice it, having a coaching culture is what's really going to turn an organization from reactive for filling leadership vacancies to proactive.

Seven Signs of a Poor Learning & Development System

These seven deadly signs, in no particular order, show a faltering development system and indicate a problem with how you're developing your people.

The company is failing to meet its business targets or objectives. There could, of course, be a number of different reasons this is happening. One key reason is that your people are not aligned with the business strategy, we talked about that previously.

But maybe they lack the talent and skills to drive the results the company needs. This comes back to our inability to develop our people. Often, when speaking with company executives in an organization either struggling in whole or in part, I find it's not that they don't have a good product or service, or even a great business plan.

It's that their people don't have the knowledge and skills to impact that business plan because they've never been coached and developed along the way. Often, I find they're victims to the Peter principle: they've promoted people in-house (which is a great tactic) but they haven't given them the additional skills they need to thrive.

There is a shortage of key talent. I hear this a lot, and I disagree. There is a shortage of willingness to develop the talent we already have. That's a critical distinction.

We have people in our workplaces who are ready, willing, and able to learn. The question is whether we are ready, willing, and able to teach them, coach them, and get them the skills they need and want to succeed.

READ
There's Really No Talent Shortage

It's a shame that when our economy turns south, one of the first things organizations cut in the budget is training. This is counterintuitive. If we believe that we train our people to make them better employees and drive more business results, why would we cut the very thing that helps our people become stronger for us during tough economic times when we need our best and brightest firing on all cylinders? Investing in training and the talent base of our people is always an investment with a high return.

Talent management is a low corporate priority. Recently, I was talking with the president of a professional services firm who looked me in the eye and said, "HR is not even on my top 10 list of things to worry about in this organization."

I said, "How can that be when HR makes up 30% of your budget?"

He had never thought about it in those terms. HR is the biggest budget item in his organization–but it's not even on his top 10 list.

This organization really has no management development program to speak of. What they called leadership development was a speaker coming in once a year for half a day. New manager orientation was a day of classroom training on computer systems and meeting other managers to understand the department interplay. That was it.

There was never a connection for the newly promoted manager of why they needed to know these things and how to apply this knowledge. This was a key component missing from the organization.

Interestingly enough, this same organization exhibited the fourth sign below.

Employee satisfaction and morale are on a downslide. This organization had taken the best places to work survey each year and every year satisfaction either held or decreased. It wasn't by a lot, but the scores were never terribly high to begin with.

Typically, when you see employee engagement on a downslide, it's because we've stopped investing in our people and in their managers. That was very true of this organization as well. The employees were telling me that their main boss (who was an owner of the company) didn't care about them as individuals and didn't see them as important cogs in what makes this organization tick.

Because that was the prevalent feeling in the organization, employees stopped engaging. They stopped trying to do their jobs at a higher level which had an impact on the customer experience.

Your employment brand is suffering. You know this is happening when you have trouble attracting quality employees. It is quite possible to have an excellent marketing brand and yet a poor employment brand.

I worked with an organization where that was true. This was a specialty regional medical practice and if you had the ailment they were known for, you went to them. They were that good. Their doctors were well-known, and they had the best and brightest in their practice.

However, their employment brand was nearly non-existent. Their own employees weren't out there telling other nurses and medical providers, "You need to come work with us and here are all the cool things about our company!" There was a dichotomy going on. The patient experience was phenomenal, and patients referred folks for care. The employment experience was not phenomenal and other employees weren't referring folks to work there. It was inhibiting their ability to develop talent in the organization.

You have problems retaining key employees. If you have low performers leaving, that's great! But if high performers and high potential employees are leaving, that's a glaring red flare in the sky for us that something is wrong with how we're managing their development.

Employees today will not be cradle-to-grave employees. We're not going to get them out of college and retain them until they retire. However, today's high potential and high performing employees crave and demand professional development opportunities and will not stay with an organization unwilling to develop them.

I have had countless owners fight me on this! They don't want to invest in employees and then the employees leave. I look at these same owners and say, "So you'd rather not have people trained and have them stay?" What are the implications of that?

Richard Branson of Virgin Atlantic is often quoted as saying, "Train your people so well that they can leave but treat them so well that they stay."

Those are profound words and yet it's an easy concept. Our people will not leave us if they feel valued, wanted, and rewarded for the efforts they give us day in and day out. It really is that simple.

Finally, the last sign is that our employment brand is tarnished. Previously, I mentioned a lack of a recruiting brand. That's fixable! But a tarnished employment brand is much more dangerous because that's really gotten to where former employees are bashing the organization on social media and telling people, "Don't go work for that company and here's why."

If your employment brand is tarnished, you're talking about having to do a complete makeover to redo your employment brand. Often, if you get on social media or sites like Glassdoor, you'll read things like "the supervisors aren't well trained" or "management doesn't respect employees." The theme is almost always there is a lack of skill set within the management function. That's always an indicator that an organization is not investing in its management development process.

Now let's look at three distinct strategies for succession planning.

Grow Your Own

One way most organizations like to succession plan is to grow their own. If you have the right culture, one with a history of developing its people and making use of its current talent pool, as well as the right people in the organization, then this is the best way to go.

It really gives us a fast track for developing our leaders versus the often costly and certainly time-consuming process of hiring from the outside and assimilating those folks into our organization.

One of the cool things about going with our own is that we can develop leaders who already understand our business. We can leverage that impact into understanding the roles in our organization. We need not explain to them how our organization makes money, what our service does, or why we provide the service we provide. They already know that. That doesn't mean they have the skill set they need to assume greater responsibility, but it does mean that we have a solid base to work on. If the right organization with the right culture already has that, then they can really streamline their succession planning process.

Make Succession Planning Important

The next thing we must do is make a case to management that succession planning is important. So even if we as C-Suite executives understand and are willing to support succession planning, we must make sure that our mid-level managers, who are often the ones driving the success of our succession plan because of their coaching efforts, understand the impact from their investment of time and often, the money of the organization in this process. One of the best ways we can do that is by developing them. If we can show them the importance of their own professional development, they'll then make it a priority to develop those below them.

I once had a manager who did not believe in developing his people. His theory was "it's not my job to teach them."

If you're a sports fan, I recall many years ago when the Green Bay Packers drafted Aaron Rogers. Brett Favre was still their quarterback. Questions were swirling around about whether Brett would soon retire, and would he transfer his knowledge?

In many interviews, Brett would say, "It's not my job to coach and develop him." That's not what a good leader says! Good leaders recognize that they have a responsibility to develop those around them.

My view on Brett's comments is that he was more concerned about his position as starting quarterback than the success of the Packers franchise. If he doesn't help this rookie assimilate into the NFL and he gets injured, the rookie is now faced with playing and Brett has done his teammates a great disservice.

WATCH
Strategic Succession Planning

While that sports analogy may not be true in every sector of business, I believe there's enough truth there because I've run into too many leaders who say it's not their job to develop folks. My view is, if you're not willing to invest in others, especially those who you manage, then you're not a true leader.

Learning & Development is a Key Business Driver

The third and final thing we can do is make learning and development a key business driver. Just like we must hold sales accountable for sales revenue and R&D accountable for innovation, we must make learning and development a key driver of our business.

This means we celebrate the contributions of our high performers and the results we're getting. If we can show our employees that management development is the centerpiece to the company's success, we will quickly become an employer of choice. The best and the brightest will not only be banging on our door, but our best and brightest will be pulling others they know into our organization.

Now we've affected our employment brand! Just like our customers come to us for high-level customer service, great employees will come to us for a great employee experience.

In the next chapter, we will look at marrying learning and development to our succession plan. This is where the magic happens!

"We need leaders who add value to the people and the organization they lead; who work for the benefit of others and not just for their own personal gain."

—MARY KAY ASH, FOUNDER, MARY KAY COSMETICS

LEARNING & DEVELOPMENT MEETS SUCCESSION PLANNING

6

Nothing is more vital to an organization's long-term health than the choice and cultivation of its future leaders. In today's business environment leaders must master general business competencies, not simply be specialists in a given area of expertise. If we will manage succession in our organization properly, we must have a flexible system oriented toward development activities.

First, let me be very clear: Learning and Development is NOT training. Training typically focuses on one-off educational events. Participants return to the workplace, and though energized, get stifled by the reality of corporate life.

I recall early in my career being sent out of town to training for three weeks. No home-time, three weeks straight of being indoctrinated into the organization's processes and culture. While exhausting, I came back ready to take on the world with this new knowledge. On my first day back, my manager asked me about the training. I relayed what I had learned and was excited to put it to use. He said, "That's great, now forget that stuff, you're back in the real world."

Wow...what a deflation! Why had I just been sent away from my family for three weeks and attended classes straight through the weekends if it meant nothing? Why would the company spend all this money on training new management folks across the country if what was being taught was irrelevant?

Effective Learning & Development

For training to really stick we must think about pairing the classroom training with real-life exposure to a variety of jobs, bosses, environments, and assignments.

Perhaps your organization can put a job rotation system in place. Typically, what happens here is an employee is allowed to work through several different types of jobs to get various perspectives on how those jobs impact the organization. What's critical in doing a job rotation as a form of development is that the employee must be held accountable for getting business results at each stop along the rotation.

It is not enough to simply check a box saying "yes" that salesperson has also been in operations and has been in the customer service telephone center, etc. For them to not only learn what they must learn but to continue to contribute to the business objectives while they're learning they must be held accountable for achieving goals during each stop in that job rotation.

Perhaps your organization isn't large enough for job rotation, think then about special assignments for people. I know several organizations that will loan out executives to the United Way for their loaned executive program. This is a great opportunity for your younger and more developing management folks to have some outside experiences, to get outside of your four walls and interact with other business professionals they may not otherwise meet.

One client had great success pulling a group of high potential employees together and giving them the opportunity to work on a very pressing business need. What was so impressive about this is that real work problems were being addressed. Work was being done inside this group leading to business problems being solved: often problems looked at from every angle by senior executives who could not come up with a solution!

If we really want to provide learning experiences for our people, often we have only to get a little creative and think about how we can engage these young up-and-coming high potentials to make sure they're developing in the way we need them to develop to continue to support the business.

Another interesting outcome that my client experienced with these "action teams" as they called them, was that it forced the people on the team to look beyond their functional silo. HR had to see things from a sales perspective, sales had to see things from a research and development perspective, and R&D had to see things from a technology perspective. This is critical, as I mentioned earlier, for today's business executives to succeed they can't simply be specialists in their own area, they must at a minimum understand how the various pieces of the business intersect and work together to provide the goods and services that the business exists to do. And when you think about it, these opportunities for our high potentials to come together are critical, especially in organizations that run lean and mean that don't have a lot of extra staff with whom these people can interact daily.

If we will do this there has to be a way to review this group's work products and its development along the way, so typically a senior member of staff or perhaps several senior executives would be in charge of working with this group to guide them, to mentor them, and then to give them feedback on their progress. This feedback also must be shared with the individuals' immediate supervisors so that when they are back in their regular jobs their supervisor can continue to incorporate the help needed areas into those high potentials' development plans.

So, if we really want to marry learning and development to our succession plan there are 10 things we need to do to make that happen.

1st: Upper management must be willing to transfer their knowledge and their experiences to the up and comers. This is a huge aid in educating and developing our future leaders. I have seen many succession plans fail at this point because the senior leaders are not willing to share their knowledge lest they become obsolete. With one particular client we solved this problem by tying the executives' bonuses partly into their ability to convey their knowledge and experiences to the younger generation of workers and to effectively mentor them. Problem solved!

2nd: We must build relationships across the generations present in our workplace. Skills, talents, and values from a diverse workforce will only strengthen our up and coming leaders, so give them exposure to folks with different perspectives than they have. Not just different perspectives in departmental responsibilities, but different life perspectives as well.

3rd: We must strengthen our leadership peer relationships. If our up-and-coming leaders see that senior leaders have built silos for themselves and are not playing in the sandbox well with each other, the message gets sent that that's the culture expected for success in the workplace. Obviously, a successful business cannot thrive if there are departmental silos. We must ask our leadership team to break those silos down so our high potentials can see their mentors working well together.

4th: We must get started on our succession plans! We can't wait until the need for the leader is obvious. At that point, the boat has left the dock! We must plan for succession years before our need. So, we not only have to develop our high potentials based on the skill sets we need today but also on the skill sets we believe we will need three, five, ten years down the road.

5th: I've talked about our high potential employees; we must identify them and then we must nurture them. These folks are usually the most likely group to leave our organization. And if the bulk of our turnover is our high potential workforce, we're dead in the water for growing our business. That means we must discover what this group of employees wants from the employment relationship and do our best to give it to them. Now, this is the point where I lose some business leaders because they'll say, "Why should I coddle this group of employees? Why shouldn't they go through the school of Hard Knocks like I had to?" In no way am I saying they shouldn't go through the school of Hard Knocks. What I am saying is that we must focus on these folks, focus on their retention, and make sure we're giving them what they need so they stay engaged in our work place and want to contribute what we're teaching them back into our work place to get the results we're looking for.

6th: In keeping with the theme of rounding out our future leaders: we must do whatever we can to provide them cross-departmental learning and exposure whether that's through the work teams we mentioned earlier or perhaps job rotation, whatever may work in your environment. It's important that this happens because it gives them an understanding and appreciation for your organization as a living system that has parts that connect together and work together.

7th: If we don't have the internal mentors that we know we need to convey knowledge to the high potential workforce, then we must consider executive coaching. There are a number of great folks at places like SCORE or private coaches who coach people for a fee. The nice thing about either option is you will get fresh ideas from people outside of your organization who aren't burdened by the culture and politics present in your organization. These folks can give your high potentials a different perspective and a different appreciation for what it means to be a leader in the workplace.

8th: As we develop our succession plans, we must include more leaders in the succession plan and what that means is that we must foster strategic thinking early in our people's career path. I do not believe that succession planning should be housed within the human resources function. A cross-section of business leaders from various disciplines contributing to our succession plan would make it a much more robust plan with better results when we need to implement it.

9th: Once we activate the succession plan and people begin to be promoted, we must be sure we've got a mentoring system in place for these folks. A high percentage of new managers fail simply because they aren't able to make that transition. Just because we've developed them and gotten them ready doesn't mean that once they take on those new responsibilities we don't continue to mentor them. This ongoing mentoring or executive coaching will help them to better acclimate into their new roles and succeed much more quickly.

Finally: We must assess our talent. What talent do we have currently? What skill sets are we lacking? Where are we going to find it? Again, I believe this assessment is not housed in HR but that our senior leadership team must assess our current talent because it will give them insights that will help them to increase their effectiveness as mentors and coaches within the organization. Nothing is more vital than that.

WATCH
What Makes
a Great Employee

At this point, you must ask yourself a few questions. What does your company value most about its leadership? What improvements would you like to see in that leadership? What is your company's philosophy about leadership? What leadership skills are crucial to your company's success? The answers to these questions will layout the road map for your succession plan.

One final thought: all of our succession planning work will be influenced by work-life concerns. We'll need to find ways to help our high potential employees balance out their work responsibilities and their personal lives. Not just because it's the right thing to do, but because the younger generations will demand it.

We also must understand the impact that generational influences will have on employees' views of career development. We want different things at various points in our careers. A young high potential who's planning a family may be ready for a move across the country now. But in a couple of years when the family has started, they may be hesitant to relocate their family and uproot their children from school systems. So, our succession plan must be a living, breathing plan. One that is flexible and can be changed. And much like I mentioned in previous chapters regarding our strategic plans, the succession plan should be dog eared, beaten up, and dirty from us taking it out and looking at it. It should be a document constantly reviewed at meetings to where succession planning becomes a part of our culture.

However, in the next chapter we'll look at how we develop a strong organizational culture that will drive business results for us.

"If you are lucky enough to be someone's employer, then you have a moral obligation to make sure people do look forward to coming to work in the morning."

—JOHN MACKEY, CEO, WHOLE FOODS

DEVELOPING AN ORGANIZATIONAL CULTURE THAT DRIVES RESULTS

7

The challenge for most business leaders with workplace culture is that they're not sure exactly what culture is, so they struggle to define theirs. The best definition of organizational culture is a pattern of shared beliefs, assumptions, values, and norms that shape the languages and practices of a group of people.

So, our staff's attitudes and the approaches they take to carry out their tasks are the tangible results of culture. The challenge with culture is that it's developed by people, usually unknowingly, and then gets transmitted to other people. This is a concept known as successive generations and in the workplace, generations are simply new employees coming into workplace.

There's an old story about a science experiment run on a group of monkeys. The monkeys were placed in a cage and some food was placed at the top of one of the tree branches.

One monkey climbed up to get the fruit and was squirted with water, so he decided he would not try to get the fruit anymore. The next day, another monkey climbed up and also got squirted. The monkeys learned that as they went up on the branch, they got squirted.

Later, the scientists brought five new monkeys into the cage. This time when one monkey went up the branch, the other monkeys were sprayed with water. Scientists eventually replaced one monkey in the group at a time. It got to where all the monkeys in the cage were new and had never been sprayed with water. Yet when one tried to climb up the branch, the others grabbed him and pulled him back down.

This is the epitome of workplace culture. The monkeys didn't know why they couldn't get the fruit, but generational knowledge passed down to them indicated that something would happen if they climbed for the fruit.

That might be a silly example, but it's exactly how culture develops in the workplace. These societal norms of what's acceptable in the workplace get handed down through successive generations of employees.

I actually had a business owner call me once and tell me he wanted to establish a workplace culture because his organization didn't have one.

I laughed because that's impossible. Every organization has a culture, whether we know it or not. This man just wasn't able to put his finger on his organization's culture. For culture to exist, all we need is that the majority of the workforce shares the norms and those norms get passed down generation to generation. The norms shape employee behavior and perceptions.

Indicators of Culture

Here's the challenge with culture: think about the old image of an iceberg with the tip of the iceberg above the water and the bulk of the iceberg underneath the surface. The same is true for culture. The things we don't see with culture are sometimes the most important, like the societal norms of the workplace, values, and shared assumptions. And like an iceberg, it's these things we need to watch out for!

What are shared assumptions? Shared assumptions are simply thoughts and feelings our employees take for granted and believe to be true.

Think about a union workforce. Often there's an "us versus them" mentality of union versus management. That's not true everywhere (many union workforces have healthy relationships with management) but there may be a perception that there has to be an adversarial relationship.

That's a shared assumption.

Values are simply beliefs employees have that specify behavior in the workplace and define what's right or wrong. Out in the world, society's morals and customs dictate how we act in public. The same is very true inside the workplace. What are the morals of the workplace? What do we define as right and wrong, acceptable and not?

Those assumptions and values turn into norms, which are unwritten rules that govern our people's behaviors.

I often get asked to come in and do culture change training. I always laugh because culture doesn't change through training or because of one event. In fact, it can take years to change an organization's culture.

Another indicator of culture are the symbols present in the workplace. Symbols are things like the acceptable attire (are we a suit-and-tie employer, are we business casual, or are we jeans and tees?), how the office is laid out (is it open? does everyone have a cubicle?), and how we celebrate (birthdays, company anniversaries, dates of hire, etc.). All of these symbols convey meaning to the people in our workforce.

READ
How to Avoid Creating a Toxic Culture

The language we use is another big one. I'm not necessarily talking about whether or not we allow four-letter words. Language is a shared system we have to generate meaning amongst our employees. Do we have lingo and/or acronyms we use to convey meaning in the workplace?

Think about any distinctive brand you may patronize. What do their symbols mean? For example, take Apple's logo. There's a significance to the bite taken out of the apple. When Apple was founded, IBM and Microsoft were the significant players on the block. Apple took a bite and look what it's become.

The Nike swoosh also conveys a certain brand–flight, forward momentum, and action. What kinds of symbols do we have in the workplace aside from our marketing brand?

What type of practices do we have? I mentioned above there might be certain symbols or ceremonies we use in the workplace but how do we celebrate employee birthdays? How do we acknowledge length of service? It's not just about celebrating major milestones in an employee's life cycle with us but how are we celebrating. That seeps into a culture as well.

Here's an example of safety culture within UPS. They recognize drivers for every year of safe driving. It starts with just a little pin for one, two years of safe driving. When you hit major milestones like five, ten, and fifteen years of safe driving there are larger awards up to where someone reaches 25 years of safe driving. At 25 years, they're inducted into the Circle of Honor, which is the UPS hall of fame that drivers strive for. They even get a jacket just like the football hall of fame inductees!

It's a big event that drivers who are members of that circle look forward to every year. That's an observable cultural custom that conveys the importance of safe driving in the organization.

Those impact and set our culture. There's a concept called socialization, which is how new employees learn those values, norms, and behaviors. It's how they're brought into the culture.

This is where a lot of organizations miss the boat when trying to change the culture in their workplace. They try to change the things we've already mentioned, the practices, customs, and ceremonies, without recognizing how socialization is affecting new people coming in.

The 4 Types of Organizational Culture

Bureaucratic culture. This type of culture is often associated with government work. Employees are governed by formal rules, SOPs, and a rigid work environment. In this culture, there is an element of stability. People know what to expect, what to do, and what buttons to push for certain results.

Organizations that thrive with a bureaucratic culture are ones that need to produce standardized goods and services like the government, fast food, and any establishment that is franchised, which needs a standardized set of operating procedures to ensure the same customer experience at every location.

Clan culture. In this culture, our employees and their behavior are shaped by traditions and loyalty to the organization besides personal commitment to the organization and a desire to be self-managed.

A clan culture typically starts to develop at the very beginning of the socialization process. Long-term employees are informal mentors in the workplace. They're the ones that either knowingly or unknowingly help socialize new employees coming in.

Often, these folks are aware of company history and know what the style and manners of conduct and behavior are. You may have heard it said, "Oh, we've always done it that way."

One danger of clan culture is folks can get into the mode of "this is how we do it" and may not be open to new ideas. But the bonus to clan culture is employees own the culture and take a lot of pride in it, so the peer pressure to adhere to the culture is strong. That can make it hard for someone with differing views about the workplace to socialize into that culture.

Market culture. Market culture reflects the significance of achieving measurable and often demanding goals. Usually, those goals are financial in nature or based on the market in which the company operates.

Companies with a market culture often focus on sales growth and profitability, and maybe market share or shareholder returns if they're a publicly traded company. Typically, in this culture, the relationship between employees and the organization is somewhat contractual.

Think of the company that preaches sales growth. Everything in their organization is likely linked to their ability to grow sales including bonuses, incentives, and base pay. Ultimately in this culture, individuals are responsible for their own performance. The organization is simply ponying up bonuses for hitting goals. This culture will thrive with people who are very self-motivated.

In this culture, managers don't get judged on their effectiveness as mentors and coaches. They're measured more on their monthly, quarterly, and annual goals that usually have something to do with profit.

Entrepreneurial culture. An entrepreneurial culture is often present in startups. This culture is characterized by a lot of experimentation, innovation, and trying to get on the leading edge of things. The organization and hence, the employees, take high levels of risk and use creativity to solve business problems.

Regardless of the culture we're in or whether we're trying to move to a different one, the culture has the potential to enhance our organization's performance. Culture can increase individual satisfaction and provides a sense of certainty about how problems are to be handled.

How to Build a Strong Culture

We see breakdowns between culture and the performance of the organization when culture is different between various functions of the organization. Culture is the control mechanism. It's what channels everyone's behaviors to the end result and weeds out undesired behaviors. But when the organization has differing sets of behaviors between functions, the employees get confused about expectations.

If we're going to build a strong culture, there are a few things we must do:

First, clean up the behavior style between functions and between management and employees. Everyone has to be on the same page with expected behaviors and behaviors we shouldn't exhibit.

Second, smooth our approaches to basic performance management, how we meet and measure goals, and how we deal with other stakeholders including customers, stockholders, vendors, and other business partners.

Third, look at the norms across the organization and make sure they're shared so they can rule how we govern rewards and punishment in the workplace.

If we can do these three things and develop a strong organizational culture, we create a stable organization that ultimately leads to a company's achievement of its strategic goals.

How do we build this strong organizational culture, especially when we think about the fact that socialization will drive it?

Know what type of culture we're trying to achieve. Which of the four types of cultures will serve us well? None are inherently right or wrong, good or bad. It's really just about what's going to work for our organization at this point in the company's life cycle.

From that, we must look at the early work assignments of new employees and ask ourselves whether they're challenging enough to help those people socialize into our culture. If not, we must redefine those jobs to make them more challenging.

This is especially critical with today's younger generations, the back end of the millennials and the front end of Gen-Z, entering the workforce. We know these folks want challenging assignments early in their careers.

Build a robust training and development program. Training and organizational development initiatives must be embedded into the culture. The things we're training and developing have to be reflected in the culture already. It's a cart before the horse situation: do we attempt to define the culture and train around it? Or do we start to train in hopes to change the culture? I don't believe there's a right or wrong way, it's just based on where the organization is at any point in time.

Reward and sustain the culture. Regardless of which we put first, the next step is to reward and sustain the culture. Rewarding key behaviors based on organizational values (such as safety, creativity, or innovation) will sustain the culture change.

Once employees see behaviors being recognized and rewarded, and the adoption of new values happens. Inherently the old behaviors, which aren't productive or conducive to the new culture, will get weeded out during the socialization process.

Redefine celebrations. Here's what's key: earlier in this chapter, I mentioned that it's not just about celebrating those things but about how they're celebrated. That's why the next step is redefining celebrations by determining the new rites and rituals we want in the organization. Though we may reward similar behaviors, it's likely time to change how we celebrate those behaviors to make sure these new celebrations fit into the new culture.

Work with role models and mentors. This final step is often forgotten. People that are early adopters of the new culture must be identified and those folks must be partnered with newer employees to help those new employees socialize appropriately.

Ultimately, if we have successfully socialized new people, we'll see job satisfaction skyrocket, greater clarity around roles and understanding of how those roles connect to the mission, and high levels of work performance. We'll see that people not only understand the culture but can articulate it and understand their role in it. We see retention increase because employees are more committed to the organization. We see the internal values of the organization morph towards the new culture.

The opposite of all those things is also true if we are unsuccessful in our new socialization attempts. Job dissatisfaction goes up. Conflict in the workplace increases. There's a sense that people lack any control over outcomes and over their jobs which leads to low performance, low engagement and ultimately a rejection of the new values.

In later chapters, we will go into even greater detail of how to impact our workplace culture. What's important to recognize here is that we have a culture and it can be changed, but those change efforts will take time. Culture can take months, perhaps even years, to change.

The longer our organization has been around with its set of norms and values, the harder it is to change. The younger we are as an organization, the easier it is to change the path of the organization.

What's important for business leaders to realize is that the benefits far outweigh the short-term pain of a lengthy organizational change process. If we're committed to changing our culture to one that will drive better organizational performance, then the change program we'll design to make the culture change happen is well worth the investment.

This starts at the work team level. In the next chapter, we'll look at how to set up our work teams for success and culture change.

"Great things in business are never done by one person. They're done by a team of people."
—STEVE JOBS, FORMER CEO, APPLE, INC.

BUILDING WORK TEAMS TO SUPPORT THE CULTURE

8

Throughout the book, we've talked about a number of different key strategies we need to employ and should expect from HR to get business results. The bottom line, however, is without the buy-in of our people and the effectiveness of teams in our workplaces none of what we've discussed can take place.

I want to bring things home with how we build effective work teams that will achieve high performance, resulting in engaged employees and teams that will further our employment brand and workplace culture.

First, we'll look at how teams develop. The word "team" is often overused. We think a group of people thrown together is a team but really a team is a group of people working together towards a common goal. Absent a common goal amongst team members, we don't truly have a team.

When I use the word "team" I want it to mean this group of people that all have a common interest in achieving shared goals.

First, we have to understand how teams develop over time.

The 4 Key Stages to Team Development

Origination, also called the forming stage, is the stage where the team comes together. It can occur when the team is initially formed, but it can also occur when a new team leader has come in, the purpose of the team has changed, or significant members of the team have changed.

Teams will move in and out of these four stages based on the members and what's happening in the workplace.

What we can't look past, however, is that the origination stage is fundamental in creating a winning team.

If we don't have measurable goals in place, if the team isn't well-trained in their duties, and if we haven't planned out the work appropriately there's no way that the team can be productive from the outset.

It's unrealistic to bring a team together and say, "here's the goal, go get 'em." We must allow the team to come together, develop its own identity, and understand how the individuals within the team will work together to allow their own personalities to come out.

Fragmentation. This stage is where a lot of teams fail. Every team goes through it, and some people call it the storming stage. This typically happens because the team is performing below expectations.

Maybe there's an over-reliance on a few key members of a team (think 20% of people doing 80% of the work sort of thing). Maybe this is the first time the team experiences conflict or negativity and doesn't know how to handle that within the group.

Whatever it is, one of the worst things that can happen within this phase is if individual members put their own achievements and goals in front of the team's performance. Every single team goes through this stage. What teams do with this stage will determine whether they can succeed in the future.

Some teams get stuck here because they can't get past infighting and conflict. If we don't get them focused on a winning culture, any initial excitement, enthusiasm, and energy we created will wane pretty quickly and productivity will suffer.

It's important to allow the team to fragment for a period of time to see if it can solve its own conflict. If it can, we will have a much more highly productive team who is going to know how to tackle big problems that come its way. If we as business leaders need to step in and help them get through the conflict, we must do that if we want results from the team.

Integration. Some call this stage where the team starts to integrate the norming stage. This is where a team moves out of conflict mode and becomes self-directed. They know they have a group of people they can trust, rely on, and work with. Now they're consistently meeting team performance targets.

As business leaders, we can step back at this point because the team is running on its own momentum now. Typically, coming out of fragmentation stage and into integration we see that the team gets more united in finding solutions to problems and there are no more rogue members putting themselves before the team.

The team gets focused on what they must do as a group to obtain their performance goals. This is the key piece in integration and it's how we know we've arrived: when each team member is supported and valued by their teammates.

That's the real determining factor of a team performing well. We typically find in the workplace that teams get to this stage when the business leader is a true coach and mentor.

As business leaders, we must allow the team to fragment but if we will get them through it, we must be willing to coach individuals and the team as a whole to get them back on track to truly integrate and perform.

The nice thing that happens here is each member of the team becomes accountable to the team for their contribution. We no longer have only a handful of members pulling their weight: everyone is contributing. An integrated team means that each team member feels empowered to make decisions that move the team forward towards it goals.

Performing. This is the most elusive stage: having a truly high performing team. Indicators we have a team in this stage are:

- The team is a cohesive unit
- The team is taking on its own identity
- Incremental performance improvements are happening (the mentality of "we hit this goal yesterday, but can we go further today")
- Resilience–when conflict comes up, they can jump over hurdles quickly and don't go back to a fragmentation stage

WATCH
Employees Must Know the Business Objectives

What we find within this team environment is very inspiring. Members want to work hard for the other members. Innovation and creativity for problem-solving is present. The team engages with each other and challenges each other professionally.

This sounds like what we want out of all teams but remember, many teams hit this stage and slip back out which may be okay. Look at any professional sports team–not every team can win the championship every year. That's what we're asking of a high-performing team: to win every year. There are examples of teams that are routinely high performing like the New England Patriots or the University of Alabama football team, but that's certainly not the norm and that's okay.

What we find is only a few teams in the workplace can probably sustain peak performance for extended periods of time unless they have a strong leader. Of the two teams I just mentioned, Alabama had Nick Saban for a number of years who is widely regarded as one of the best college football coaches. The Patriots have Bill Belichick who is widely regarded as one of the best pro football coaches of all time.

Our goal as leaders should be to get every team to integrate. It takes a unique group of members to play off each other's strengths to sustain a level of high performance. It requires a bit of magic sauce to get the team into high performance and keep them there.

As leaders, we must look at each team present in our workplace and ask: where are they currently? Can we look at our work groups and label them as being in one of these four stages? If so, what is it going to take to move them to the next key stage? What must we do as leaders to coach and mentor them? Do we need to change personnel in the team?

The one thing I beg of you is to not do some sort of team-based activity where we take an underperforming team, send them to a ropes course for the day, and think the problem is solved.

It's certainly a fun day out of the office but it rarely changes performance. I once saw a cartoon of this adage that showed four executives in an airplane with parachutes on and the plane door open. The leader is saying, "to improve our teamwork, only three of the parachutes will open."

That's why these team event type things don't work. They are fun, don't get me wrong. I believe they have a place in engaging employees, giving them opportunities to bond and reflect on each other's personalities, and developing memories together. But I'm not convinced those activities actually create a more cohesive team unit.

Supporting Your Team at Each Stage

The question with these four stages is: what do we have to do to support our team in each one?

Throughout Origination, the key focus for us is to provide clear direction for the team. We must help them set their purpose and vision, develop goals, and guide them in how the team should be structured with roles within the team.

We cannot do this for the team. Instead, we must provide clear direction on those things. It's important for us to remember that if we step in and do things for the team, the team will never get out of the first stage.

In Fragmentation, the focus becomes continuing to provide clear direction, but now we may need to step in to support a little more. We have to recognize that they are in conflict and while we want them to resolve that conflict to the best of their abilities, we can't let them flounder either. A good leader must know when it's time to step back in and provide support.

We can work with them on coming back to their values by revisiting the values the team has set, asking the team to reevaluate behaviors exhibited by members, to reassess team responsibilities, and to go back to the measures we're using to define team performance.

We may find that the responsibilities team members have assigned to one another is part of the problem. Maybe we're not utilizing some of the team member's best skill sets in their current role and it's time to shake up member responsibilities to get through this stage.

When Integrating, our role as a business leader changes yet again. Here, our support for the team must be focused on getting them to explore innovative ways to improve efficiencies.

How can they be more effective in individual responsibilities? They may need help with holding each other accountable, communicating within the team unit, and it is certainly time for the team to show appreciation and recognition for each other's contributions. There is a shift away from us as cheerleaders to the team being their own cheerleaders. We don't stop cheering, but we encourage that within the team members as well.

During High performance, the team needs us to help them prioritize KPIs. This is one thing that's going to contribute to real sustained success, and we must help the team define those things and empower them to make the decisions that will affect those KPIs.

Here we want them to take ownership of their own behavior. We're there supporting them, but the momentum they're gaining is gained more by their own internal structure than it is from us as a leader.

Our biggest role for them is to keep nudging them in incremental performance improvements. We can keep stretching the goals for them and keep them challenged so they don't get complacent.

What are the implications for us as leaders at each stage?

At Origination, we must have a more directive approach and guidance. We must show the team how the process will develop and help them with laying down a clear structure. Often, members will take the wait-and-see approach and their elected leader may lead for the time being.

For us, we must make sure that the processes of the team are driven by their team leader. We must allow the leader to make things happen. We also must remember that some people on the team may not be comfortable yet. They may be reluctant to openly contribute to discussions because trust still must be built. Allow that trust to develop amongst members at the pace with which they're comfortable.

Whoever their nominated leader is, we must let them make some decisions. We may want to remind the team that just because someone is vocal and outspoken, that doesn't make necessarily make them a leader and we want to make sure that person doesn't dominate all discussions.

In Fragmentation, the implications change again. I mentioned above we need to be supportive and actively listen to members. They may come to us with concerns, may need help managing conflict, and may openly ask for support.

In this stage, their nominated leader may be under more pressure to pull the team together so the coaching and mentoring of their leader take precedence during this stage. We may need to allow the processes they're working on to break down to get the conflict resolved.

This is a hard one for a lot of leaders who want to step in to ensure no mistakes are made. But if the implications for the business aren't dire, we may need to allow their processes to break down to work through conflict. This is where the trust factor comes out. We'll see smaller

WATCH
Play to Your Key Talent

groups within the team form trust and as that happens, trust forms between groups and runs into the rest of the team.

We must be careful in mentoring the team at this stage. It's sometimes hard for them to make decisions and they may rely too much on compromise instead of making the decisions that will push forward to achieving results. Our responsibility as leaders at that time is to again keep them focused on the big picture. It's not about making every team member happy, it's about doing what's best for the business.

That leads us back to the Integration stage. Here, the team leader is now respected as a team member. There may be some shared leadership. Maybe there are some processes other team members are allowed to lead and that's perfectly okay. Our role at this point is to help develop consensus. We want to help the team make decisions everyone is engaged in and can get behind.

At this stage, mutual respect occurs between the leader and the rest of the team. The team looks to the leader for guidance and trust them to take the team where it needs to go.

When the team is at this stage, the core processes that were such a struggle before operate smoothly. As leaders, we can step away now because we're seeing the team coalesce.

As they accept roles within the team and their roles continue to clarify, trust and relationships take over. There's no longer as much of a tentative relationship with the "wait-and-see" mentality. They're beyond that now and trust is implicit within the team.

As we come out of decision-making mode, we find the team looks for win-win opportunities. Instead of giving some things up they ask, "How can we achieve everything we all want to achieve?" Creativity and innovation come to the forefront.

As leaders, we must allow that creativity and innovation to take place even if there are ideas we know won't work. It's imperative that the team come to that conclusion on their own if we want to get them to the high-performance stage.

At High Performance, our role changes to one of overview. We need not be in the day-to-day of the team anymore because we've mentored them through each stage and can see a shared leadership within the team. They're placing more trust in the leaders of the various processes of the team. We also see more personal relationships develop and that helps to support the leadership structure. When you genuinely like someone as an individual, you respect them as a team leader.

Since process functions are going well at this point, as leaders we're simply watching for their ability to make minor adjustments as needed to get more performance and productivity out of their own process.

Finally, we'll find that their decision making becomes easier, quicker, and folks may even trust individuals within the team to make decisions in the team's best interest. When the football team has a high performing quarterback, they no longer must rely on the coach to send plays in. The team trusts the quarterback to call the plays at the line of scrimmage. That's exactly what we're talking about in workplace teams.

How to Build a Team Destined to Become High Performing

How do we build a team destined to become a high performing team? There are nine steps and each weaves their way through those four stages.

Establish the purpose, meaning, and vision. This is the first point of building a solid team and it's often the most overlooked step. But if we complete it, it really helps pull the team together. If they know exactly why they've formed, their goals, and what the team is supposed to be doing, that eliminates a lot of the conflict right from the start.

Establish values and behaviors. If we don't set expectations within the team early on, we will allow unwanted behaviors to forever permeate through the team's performance and decision-making process.

Establish roles and the structure of the team. Who's going to do what within the team? It's important here we allow the team to nominate its own leader they want to follow.

It's also critical that the structure of the team reflects what it must accomplish. I was recently working with a board of directors in the conflict/fragmentation stage on this topic. I found that the structure and definition of roles within the board were not present. They had multiple members on and chairing different committees and there was such a spiderweb of interconnectedness that no one knew who was in charge of what. Setting roles and structure early in the team's development is critical to the success of the team.

Create goals and measures. As leaders, we must allow the team to set its own goals and decide how it will measure its progress. We'll offer guidance and expectations, but let's let them go after it in their own way. Out of that will come a shared sense of responsibility among team members. They'll work harder towards any goal they develop than they would towards any goal we develop for them.

Develop the team based on the situation. Not every team progresses at the same rates and times. Our role as leaders must change based on what stage the team is in and the issues they're facing. Our role as leaders will also change based on who makes up the team. For example, a team of younger employees may need different leadership than a team of people who have been with our organization for a long time.

Create communication strategies. What is the best way for the team to communicate their successes, challenges, and a need for decision making? This piece is critical in today's environment of remote work teams. How are we going to allow them to contribute and how are they going to contribute across time zones, continents, and geographies? We might think we know what's best for them, but again we must allow them to determine what's best for them and their needs.

Provide resources. This is our job as leaders. No team can perform to its full potential without resources. In my work I often hear from team members, "we could get so much more done if we only had the authority to make decisions" or "if we only had a budget that we controlled" or "if we only had the tools to do the work."

We cannot give employees every possible thing they want but if we're expecting the team to achieve results without the proper resources to achieve them, they will fail, and we'll demotivate them.

Empower them to make decisions. We've given them the rules of the game and the resources they need so it's time to step back and let them know that they have the authority to make decisions to achieve the business results we've all agreed on.

Celebrate their success. Show appreciation and recognition for jobs well done. One of the most overlooked and powerful forms of employee recognition is peer recognition. People appreciate recognition from their team members, their peers, even more so than from a manager or supervisor.

To establish a team, we must allow it to go through the four stages and we must focus on those nine key points to allow them to progress through those stages. We must know as leaders what the team and team leaders need from us at any point in time. If we do those things, we're setting the stage for establishing a teamwork culture.

So, you say you've got a high performing team? Time to integrate that into your company culture! In the next chapter, I will outline how to turn your culture into one of teamwork that achieves business results.

"Alone we can do so little; together we can do so much."

—HELEN KELLER, AUTHOR AND ACTIVIST

ESTABLISHING A CULTURE OF TEAMWORK

9

We often hear about the importance of teamwork in the workplace. To be clear, it is critical in today's global economy that we're able to work well in all kinds of teams, including teams across time zones and continents.

Regardless of where we find our teams, there are a couple of key steps we must follow to achieve high performance within those teams.

Communication. Are executive leaders clearly communicating that teamwork and collaboration are expected, and that no one completely owns a work area or process by themselves? Are they communicating that the process owners must be open to input from others on the team?

It's the age-old adage that leaders must lead by example. They must establish their expectations early in the process and the leadership team must demonstrate those same expectations.

Modeling. Work teams must look at the executive team and see they too function as a team. They must see how the executive team interacts with one another and how they're open to input from one another.

This is especially critical when things go wrong. It's easy to get along and work well together when everything going fine. But as we know in business there are challenges and hurdles that must be overcome. That's when work teams really need to come together to avoid unfriendly behavior, the blame game, and perhaps even backstabbing.

We've talked quite a bit about culture throughout this book and that's the next thing we have to analyze for really good teamwork.

Culture. Do members of the team value culture in the workplace and value teamwork? One of the best things we can do when forming a new team is getting them to agree on team values and make sure those values get written down.

Once we set the stage for teamwork, it's important to remember rewards and recognition.

Recognition. We must build in recognition and perhaps bonuses that are team-based. We want to get out of the mode of the lone ranger where the lone ranger is praised and rewarded for moving away from the team towards their own agenda and goals. There has to be a compensation and rewards system in place that acknowledges collaboration while also honoring the individual contribution to the team.

Folklore. This is often overlooked and falls into the scope of bringing people together. Folklore is the things that bring people together, the stories they share, how the company is helping them grow as individuals, how they're helping each other to grow, and that sense of camaraderie they create.

It's important to allow a team to develop that sense of camaraderie on their own because it can't be forced. As they develop, they'll create the things that bind them. Let's allow them to have those experiences and relive those moments together.

Performance Management. This is the final piece. Have a performance management system that emphasizes and values teamwork. Often, one of the best systems to do this is some type of 360-degree feedback system that ensures we're getting that valuable input from our peers who are our team members.

Leadership must drive all six items and has to be very conscious of the fact that while they're driving them, they should have a bit of a hands-off approach. The team must be allowed to go through the phases we've discussed and to fight their own struggles. As business leaders, we are responsible for setting that stage.

READ
Forbes: How to Change Your People's Behavior

Often, executives want team training to take place but what they really want is a group of people to come together to solve a problem. So that's what the training should be about.

We need not train people on how to work together. Adults will figure out how to work together if they agree on the things we've mentioned including the values, norms, and the compensation system. Our training should focus on methods of project management and problem-solving so the team spends its energy on those things, not on figuring out how to work together.

We must be wary of having meetings to have meetings. Let's allow the team to decide the point at which a project isn't moving forward at the rate it needs to be and figure out where it's failing in its own processes. Often projects are held up not because of individual personalities but because members haven't agreed on the steps required to move forward. As leaders, perhaps we need to facilitate that rather than having a status update meeting.

One thing that's critical to team development is allowing them to build fun into the processes, whether that means allowing them to get together over lunch or leave the office to go someplace else to work on the project. Whatever they define as fun, this creates a shared experience amongst the team which again goes back to developing that folklore and sense of community within the team. Let's allow the team members to be the best they can be in the environment that promotes them being the best they can be.

I would even suggest beginning each team's session with a different team member coming up with problem-solving icebreakers. It need not be corny but let them come up with some little thing that will allow them to let their hair down and get a little relaxed before jumping right back into problem-solving mode. This small investment of time lets members get to know each other better over the course of time.

Obviously, we must allow teams to celebrate their successes. Do they want t-shirts saying, "Hey we did it"? Do they want a free lunch on the company or an extra day off? The key is to allow them to tell you how they want to celebrate their wins rather than assuming!

As leaders, if we can do these team exercises, we'll be amazed at the progress we'll make not just on business goals but on creating a culture of teamwork where each person has a contribution to the team.

Myths Around Teams

I want to shift gears a bit and talk about myths around teams.

Adventure learning. This is the myth that adventure learning, where teams go off go to a ropes course or play paintball, creates strong teams. Those aren't inherently bad activities, but teams don't fail because they have fears or cannot trust other members. Teams fail because the members are confused about their roles or level of authority or what the team's mission really is.

Adventure learning activities are fun and help develop folklore, but they're not designed to truly improve teamwork in the workplace.

Personality type. To be sure, there are various personality assessments and they have their place if they're used appropriately. The problem is that teams don't fail because they have different personalities. They rise and fall based on how members behave toward one another.

These assessments only go so far. They measure nothing that truly matters to the team, they measure how we are as individuals. We must recognize that there's a limit to what these tests can do for teamwork.

Personality assessments can come in handy in allowing members to recognize how each other is seen. But they cannot and should not be used to ensure that everyone on the team has the same personality.

People like working together. This is one of my favorites. Some people thrive in groups. Obviously, others do not. We cannot expect that the team is in constant contact with one another–it's okay for them to break off and work solo occasionally as long as they're working solo towards the team's goals.

Some people want to maintain their individual identity. Let's honor that. We never need to ask members to give up their individual identity for the sake of the team identity. This is a fine line especially when we're talking about working with team members across technology because people need to have access to one another but that doesn't mean they must be in constant physical contact with one another. People need alone time as well.

Teamwork is more productive than individual work. Teams are inherently inferior to individuals in terms of efficiency. Individuals don't have to develop consensus. Teams aren't as time efficient, however highly functioning teams get better results than individuals because of the varied viewpoints present. Teamwork may actually take a bit longer to get to the results, but the results are better.

The more the merrier. Smaller teams are usually better. There's no magic number for team size, but there are some things to think about.

Start by considering the core team members. These folks are 100% dedicated to the goals the team is working towards. There are other folks with whom they may need to interact, perhaps some support people from other departments, but that doesn't mean the providers of information must be on the team.

If we're not careful about the number of people on the team, we quickly not only have a massive team but also end up in a situation where people are going to team meetings but have nothing to do at them. That's the definition of being unproductive.

7 Keys to An Effective Team

1. Team members share leadership roles. Each team member champions one piece of the project.
2. The team develops its own scope of work. After all, they have their focus and goals from leader-

ship so it's their job to figure out what to do to get results.

3. The team schedules their own work and takes the time to do it. Within the guidelines we've given them, we must allow them to work as a team when and how they need to.
4. Tangible work products come out of the team. If that's not happening or it's not happening on a timely basis, we don't have an effective team.
5. The team has individual members who are mutually accountable for results. No one person can drive everything and no one person can hold the team back. Individuals must work together to get results and manage each other so everyone is contributing.
6. The team's performance is focused on achieving team products, not individual successes.
7. Problems are discussed and resolved by the team. There's no backstabbing or running to managers to resolve problems.

If you have a work group that can exhibit those seven characteristics, I'll show you a work group knocking it out of the park for you.

Knowing what effective teams look like, how do we develop one as leaders?

The first thing we must do is sit down with the team and establish objectives together. We work with them to define performance measures and make sure all team members understand them and will commit to them. If they aren't, we may need to find new members for the team.

Second, we must instill in the team a participatory style, so they feel open to suggesting ways to improve

READ
The Shape of Leadership

the goals of the team and work products of the team as well as developing an environment in which members acknowledge the validity of one another's viewpoints.

Next, focus on contributions. Here we must have the team define its objectives for how each member is going to actively contribute to the team. This allows us as leaders to not only hold the team accountable for achieving the work product but hold members accountable for their roles in the product.

The fourth item is to help members organize their meetings. You can meet with the whole team and encourage members to discuss their concerns. Eventually, leaders may not need to attend meetings, but we'll want to help them get organized initially and guide them through the storming process that will eventually come.

The next thing is to organize the members and establish clear roles. Once each member fully understands their role and is committed to it, the less likely members are to become frustrated.

When we see people checking out of a team project, it typically comes back to them not understanding their own role or perhaps another member taking their role from them.

Next as leaders, we allow the team to develop its rules. What standards are being established within the team and what's the rationale for those standards? We must be involved as leaders to make sure rules and standards don't conflict with the work product and the goals the team is ultimately charged with achieving.

Then, we must promote team responsibility. This is where we encourage each member of the team to take responsibility for completing specific tasks and bringing solutions–in other words, being an active participant in the team.

Finally, our role as leaders is to help the team establish time commitments. How will they schedule meetings? Will they devote individual time to work on pieces of the project? What monitoring processes will the team put in place to ensure they're staying on task?

In today's work environment, very few jobs can be achieved successfully individually. So, whether our teams are formally defined and long-term or they're more informal and short-lived projects, the steps and concerns we've talked about in this chapter must be followed if we want to be certain that the team is getting the results we're expecting of them.

Like any other culture, a team-based culture is fragile. If we don't continually nurture it, it will go away. If we don't follow the steps outlined in this chapter, we're in danger of creating an environment where everyone wants to be on a team for the sake of being on a team whether they have input or not. That environment will slow down progress immensely.

As leaders, our role ultimately comes back to setting the stage. Are we working well with fellow executives? Are we exhibiting team behaviors ourselves? If so, that sets the stage for a teamwork culture moving down through the rest of the organization.

Now that we've created the culture we want, let's look at how to use culture to drive employee engagement.

"Research indicates that workers have three prime needs: Interesting work, recognition for doing a good job, and being let in on things that are going on in the company."

—ZIG ZIGLAR, AUTHOR AND MOTIVATIONAL SPEAKER & ACTIVIST

CREATING A CULTURE OF ENGAGEMENT

10

When we think about workplace culture, it seems like an ambiguous term. We hear it a lot and often folks aren't quite sure what it means. Remember the business owner I previously mentioned who said his workplace had no culture?

It's easy to imagine that workplace culture is based on how people interact with each other. What we must understand is how culture impacts employee engagement. What is the relationship between culture and the employee's level of commitment to the organization and their performance in driving business results?

Most of us would like to have an organization where employees say they love their jobs, and we all want to work in organizations where we love our jobs. Ultimately, while it may seem like a pie-in-the-sky goal, having our employees love their jobs is just the beginning of identifying the kind of culture we want.

WATCH
Balancing the Employee Relationship

Many things go into employees loving their jobs, some of which are out of our control as leaders. However, that's where we'll start.

A study was done by Gallup that looked at employee commitment and engagement levels. The results?

Only 29% of respondents said they love their job. Note that someone who loves their job is typically someone who is engaged.

A whopping 54% said they do "just enough to get by and get paid." They're showing up, punching the clock, and keeping their heads down all in the name of grabbing a paycheck at the end of the week.

That leaves us with 17% of respondents and unfortunately, this is the statistic that's really scary: 17% of respondents are actively disengaged. These folks are probably not only underperforming, but they really don't care that they're underperforming. They have completely checked out.

This means that 70% of our people are not engaged in today's workforce. That may not be true of your particular workplace at this point in time, but I would encourage you to take an honest look at the state of your workforce and ask yourself how closely those numbers reflect what's happening in your organization.

Besides engagement, I want to look at two other terms: commitment and morale. Most times they go hand in hand, but they are slightly different. Commitment is someone's loyalty to their workplace–their devotion or dedication. Do they believe in what the organization is doing?

Morale, on the other hand, is a mental or emotional condition such as "I'm enthusiastic" or "I'm confident" regarding what they have to do in the organization. That's where these two terms are slightly different. Someone can be fully committed to your organization because of the services you're delivering or products you're manufacturing, but morale may still be low because there's a lack of common purpose regarding their teammates.

This is a very important distinction for us to consider and one that's often missed in employee opinion surveys. When I review the results of employee opinion surveys for clients, I typically see lines of questioning around one of these areas, but not both.

When we focus on one area, such as low morale, but we fail to follow up and ask if the person is committed to where we are, we miss out. Sometimes a disconnect of team experience from where the company is going drives morale down.

I've talked to so many people who have left organizations they were proud to work for because either their manager could not keep them motivated or they didn't like the team they were working with. Commitment wasn't lacking, but morale was taking such a hit they needed to find that enthusiasm elsewhere.

When it comes down to it, engaged employees are emotionally and mentally invested in their work and are committed to contributing to employer success. This is all about morale and commitment. So ultimately the way to drive engagement, as we'll see, is allowing our people to bring all of themselves to work every day.

The Corporate Leadership Council completed a study on the engagement level of 50,000 employees around the world. I wasn't surprised to see they found that the employees who are most committed to their organizations perform 20% better and are 87% less likely to leave their employers.

These numbers shouldn't be surprising to anyone. We see these types of numbers all the time in various studies surrounding employee engagement. But I emphasize this study because I want you to think about what it would be like to get 20% better performance out of your workforce and what that would mean to your organization. What would that mean to the customers you're serving, what would that mean for your ability to give back to the community and to provide an even better experience for your employees? What could you do with 20% better results?

What is Culture Anyway?

Let's look at the other side of the equation: our culture. Culture is typically defined as the values and behavioral norms present within an organization.

It's kind of like our DNA, what makes us tick. Some people call culture "the way we do things around here." Those ways of looking at culture have merit.

One of the biggest drivers of culture is obviously management. What management pays attention to and rewards daily is the strongest indicator of an organization's culture.

We may say to our people that customer service is the most important thing we have to offer our customers but if daily we rate our people on their level of output and their productivity, there's a disconnect. Here, we don't really have a culture of customer service, we have one of being highly productive.

Perhaps that high-level production helps us meet our customer service focus but if our people don't make that connection, they will perceive a disconnect in the culture.

I invite you to think about these seven things when it comes to culture in your organization:

1. What words would you use to describe your organization or your team?
2. How are decisions made in your organization?
3. How are promotions determined?
4. What aspect of the business is focused on the most?
5. What gets rewarded?
6. What does your physical environment look like?
7. How is feedback given?

If you are able to answer those seven questions honestly and with an open mind, you'll get a picture of what culture is present in your workforce right now.

For instance, if you believe you have a very participative culture in which employees are able and willing to share ideas and provide input but you said decisions are made solely by the C-suite and output is rewarded more than brainstorming, then you don't really have an open and participative culture.

As business leaders, we often have rose-colored glasses on when we think about our culture. Even if we don't have the glasses on, we often forget how important culture is to the achievement of business results.

I was working with a business owner recently who said that he knew he needed to work on his culture. Through the course of chatting with his employees and facilitating focus groups, he knew that employees were mostly happy working there. The business also had low turnover.

It was a professional services environment and a very creative organization. He allowed people to come to work dressed comfortably–business casual at best, though he himself would wear business attire.

What I found was lacking were just simple things. Here's one that stands out–his people said they would like more of an opportunity to work remotely. After all, in their business creativity is key. So why not let the employees work where and when they can be at their most creative?

As I talked with the owner, he laughed and said, "Ed, I don't get these young people. Why are they so insistent on working from home?"

I laughed and said, "What would it cost you to allow that a few days per week? What would that really cost you?"

He said, "Nothing really."

So, if your people are asking for it and it's not a financial burden, why wouldn't you do it?

Whether or not we as leaders think something is important, if our people are asking and it might make the workplace just a little better for them, why wouldn't we do that? Why wouldn't we listen to them on these types of things? These are golden nuggets of building the culture we want to build in our organization.

WATCH
Things That Make You Go Hmmm

So often you read that culture is this big, nebulous idea. I'm a believer that culture is in all the little things done well. I believe it's the little things we do for our people that build a culture that drives business results. The problem is that most leaders fail to recognize the little things that are actually working.

With this, little things can also cause a disconnect. So, we must be careful! For instance, I worked as a consultant within a professional services firm for a number of years. In my role I had regular contact with all the members of the HR team.

As part of their culture, greeting cards would be on a person's desk when they arrived for work on their birthday. These cards were sent out by HR. I arrived at my desk one year to a card addressed to "Michael Krow." Now, to be clear, that is my given first name, but I never used it. Everyone in my life knows me as Ed. That's a disconnect.

The person in HR in charge of this activity knew me well but didn't take a moment to put my common name on the card. Turns out, several other employees had the same experience.

This is such a little thing, but it's related to culture. If you have a culture of informality and teamwork, and you can't get names correct, the message is off.

Just like the nuggets of building great culture are in little things, as the saying goes, the devil is also in those details.

The importance of culture is that culture drives employee engagement. Until we get employees engaged, we cannot be a high performing organization. It's impossible.

If you go back to the Gallup study that showed only 29% of the workforce is truly engaged, it's not a logical leap to say we can't possibly be a high performing organization if only 29% of our people are committed.

There's a direct link from culture to high performance. We can't have a bad culture and a high performing team because a bad culture will not drive engagement and without engagement, there is no high performance.

The Levels of Employee Engagement

When we think about employee commitment to us, there are two levels: external and internal. Both lead to employee engagement with us.

External commitment is driven by the things that bring people to us for employment. Perhaps they know of our brand in the marketplace. Perhaps it's a position they've always wanted. Perhaps the pay is right for them. These are the external things that make them say, "I will apply for work there."

If through the course of the interview they believe these external commitments can be met and we believe their talents are a match for us, we shake hands and embark on the employment relationship. However, they're not yet engaged. This is the point at which we can make or break engagement.

This is where we must get them internally committed to us.

Internal commitment makes them get out of bed every day and say, "I love my job, I love the work we're doing in the community, I love my employer, I love the products we put out."

That level of internal commitment is driven by the culture they experience once they're in the workplace.

I was disheartened during a recent project for a financial institution with serious financial troubles who wanted help looking at their staffing models. As I was interviewing several key members of the management team, I was also trying to figure out what was going on with the market brand.

I asked one of the key management people what differentiated her institution from others.

She said, "I can't think of anything really."

That speaks to culture.

I followed it up with, "Let's say you and I are at a picnic and we start talking about work. Would you recommend I come to work here?"

Her response?

"Absolutely not."

She said, "Actually, Ed, I wouldn't even tell you where I worked."

This is an unfortunate sign of an extremely dysfunctional culture. I say that because it didn't stop with this high-level management person—not a single key employee I spoke to would recommend their best friend come to work there.

It's no wonder this organization is in serious trouble.

There is zero engagement by the workforce in the mission of this institution. It's the perfect example of why we must care about our culture and engaging our employees.

The book *First, Break All the Rules* by Marcus Buckingham, contains a quote I find I refer to often with my clients: "You can't motivate other people. You can only influence what they're motivated to do."

There's a lot of wisdom in that quote. I work with many organizations on engagement and motivation, but the truth of that quote is that we can't focus on the person. We must focus on getting them to do what we need them to do. Those are two different things.

I would love for every employee to be happy. But I will take having every employee be committed to my business and motivated to do what they do. Those are two different goals, and you have to ask yourself which one is more important. They're not mutually exclusive but in the event they are, which one is more important?

Do you think that the average NFL player enjoys spending all the time in the weight room that they do to get the physique needed to play 16 games a year?

Probably not! But that's where the real work is.

Do we motivate them on how much weight they can lift? Or do we motivate them on our goal to get to the Super Bowl?

Again, those are two different messages.

One is focused on individual accomplishment. The other is focused on a much longer-term prize in which not only the individual wins but the team wins. If we get our people focused on the Super Bowl, they'll do the things they need to do to strengthen themselves to contribute to the victory.

Steven Covey defines motivation as a fire from within. He says that if someone else tries to light the fire under you, it will burn only briefly.

That speaks volumes about why we must motivate people around a common goal and not try to motivate them individually. Motivation certainly comes from within, but it builds from within because of the interesting and challenging work we provide to our people.

Ultimately, this is based around a person's desire to grow not only as a person but as a professional in their line of work.

There are three commonly accepted steps on the motivation ladder:

1. We shake hands with a candidate, and both of us agree that they will share their time, talent, and efforts to drive our business results. They believe that the pay and benefits we offer them will allow them to put food on their table, a roof over their head, etc. They have probably met their supervisor during the process and will feel comfortable working with that person.

2. Once they get their feet wet in the organization, now we get into some of the short-term motivation things like bonuses, company awards, and birthday celebrations. I call these the easy things to go after. Who doesn't like to be recognized for their service and get cake on their birthday? These make someone proud to work for you.

But the associated motivation is short-lived. Last month's birthday cake doesn't make someone focused on doing their job well today.

What does it take to get to the final step of sustained motivation?

3. This is what we need to focus on that so many businesses don't: the importance of the work itself. How proud is someone to do work they do for your organization? What level of responsibility do they have? What are social interactions like? Do they get along with their supervisor and teammates? What opportunities are present for them to grow and advance? Do they get a sense of achievement out of what they do?

These are higher-level things that take time, thought, and effort around developing in an organization. If we will maintain a motivated workforce, we have to focus on these high-level things. They drive commitment over time because through them, we're meeting the more advanced needs of our employees. It's like Maslow's hierarchy of needs: we all need basic things first before worrying about the high-level pieces.

In terms of employee motivation in the workplace, it's not that dissimilar. Once someone is satisfied with their paycheck, they'll start looking for more things that will drive them. It's critical that we focus on these things if we want a high performing organization.

An organization called Peak Performance conducted studies on what a high performing, motivated workforce really looks like. They found when conducting performance reviews that more than a third of employees consistently exceeded performance expectations. The average worker in a high performing organization performs better than the industry average of similar workers doing similar work.

These employees have strong emotional commitments to the workplace, whether it's a commitment to the vision of the organization or to their coworkers. In the best-case scenario, it's both.

The study also found that individual departments were also performing at high levels.

WATCH
The 2 Biggest Demotivators

Finally, the thing they found I think is most important is that high performing organizations have leaders who believe their front-line people are the key to their success and they work diligently to engage these people on an emotional level.

I'd ask you to stop for a minute and ask yourself to think about your workplace. Do you meet any of those criteria? How far away from a high performing culture are you?

Manpower commissioned a study where they asked employees about the things that mattered to them that their companies are not doing well. There were five key areas:

1. Feeling appreciated for the work they do.
2. A stressful environment. (People don't want to work in a stressful environment. That doesn't mean the work isn't stressful, but the environment shouldn't be.)
3. Feeling valued and respected within their immediate work group and the organization as a whole.
4. Career opportunities for advancement.
5. The organization effectively utilizing their knowledge and skills.

I look at these five areas and they're not that hard. I don't think there's an "ah-ha" moment in there for anyone. Yet this study showed that employees are saying "we want this, and the company is not providing it." To me, that's a shame because these are such easy fixes for us.

Remember earlier when I said the golden nuggets are in the little things? These are little things we can do!

Not surprisingly, about a third of people quitting their jobs are quitting because of a lack of or limited appreciation for contributions. I'm sure some readers are saying "I thought people leave because of their supervisor?" Well...who's the one who should be showing appreciation for their contributions?

This comes back to the culture of the organization. If the culture is one where giving regular feedback and recognizing accomplishments isn't valued or measured, of course, supervisors won't perform those activities. There's the start of your motivation problem.

Yet another Gallup survey (often called the Gallup dozen survey) came up with 12 things employees want from the workplace that will help drive commitment (in no particular order):

1. To know what's expected of them at work.
2. To have everything they need to do their work.
3. The opportunity to do what they do best every single day.
4. Recognition or praise within the last seven days.
5. To work for an organization and individual who cares about them as a person.
6. An environment where development is encouraged.
7. Their opinions to matter.
8. The organization's mission makes them feel like their job is important.
9. To work with coworkers who are also committed to doing quality work.
10. To have a best friend at work (this one surprised me!).

11. Their supervisor to have talked to them about their progress within the last six months.
12. Opportunities to learn and grow this year.

When I look at this list, I'm hard-pressed to find any of those twelve things I wouldn't want myself. I think if we're honest with ourselves, these things are important. If we delivered these twelve things to our people, what kind of difference would that make in the workplace culture?

If you look at the theme in those twelve items, people are telling us that the most powerful motivator is personalized recognition from their manager for a job well done. They want a manager who appreciates their effort and will thank them for those efforts.

We know that achievement and recognition are primary employee motivators in the workplace. Folks want to go home feeling like they accomplished something that day and they want to be recognized for those accomplishments.

When it comes to achievement, no one is motivated by the threat of failing. Very few people are working hard because they're so scared of failure they want to succeed. They work hard because of the promise of achieving something—whether or not that comes with some bonuses or pay increases. Those things are external motivators. It's that sense of achievement we're striving for out of our people.

I worked with a client recently looking at pay disparities in their organization. One stood out to me: the CEO said about an employee, "It doesn't matter that she's underpaid. She's never leaving here."

Aside from the fact that it's wrong that she's underpaid, he conveyed that she loves her job and the organization so much she probably doesn't care that she's underpaid.

To be clear, I'm not advocating for this. I'm advocating for having people who are that committed to our organization, but we must reward them for that as well. We cannot expect that someone fired up for our organization will continue to have that passion if they don't feel appreciated and rewarded for their efforts.

Achievement really means two things: either the employee has done something for the first time and is excited about having done it for the first time or they did something better than ever done before (think of the salesperson who breaks $1MM in sales for the first time or lands a Fortune 500 client for the first time).

But if we don't recognize them for their achievement, it's all for naught. Recognition is simple, and the most satisfying and effective way to offer ongoing recognition to our people is through one-on-one feedback. It's the supervisor who is willing to say simple things like "thank you" for a job well done or "you hit the ball out of the park today."

This isn't rocket science!

I'm sure some of you are reading this saying, "Gee, Ed, I've heard all this before." Then I challenge you to think about why it's not happening in your workplace.

It's often said that the biggest gap in performance is the gap between what we know we should be doing and what is actually being done. We know recognition is crucial and yet we rarely have the infrastructure in organizations to provide that feedback regularly to our people.

I'm willing to bet this is what's going on in your business: the average employee assumes if they hear nothing from their supervisor, no news is good news and they'll be told if something is wrong.

I'm willing to bet that negative reinforcement is common–when they mess up, their supervisor jumps on them right away for it. I bet the positive reinforcers that may be present are not directly connected to the mission of the organization and the person's job duties.

Worst of all, you may be in the flavor of the month club where there are constant redirection and correction and changing of course for employee duties.

When we're in that kind of environment, here's what happens to employees–they succeed, they have an achievement, they tell themselves, "Wow, I did it." They get no response from their supervisor and after a couple days go by, they start to think, "Hmm, I think that's how I was supposed to do it but now I'm not sure."

Now, they're not smiling anymore, they're perplexed. As time goes on with still no response, inevitably their attitude becomes, "well, I guess it doesn't matter if I do it or not."

That's where disengagement starts. Behavior that goes unrecognized will go extinct.

That's actually true throughout the animal kingdom as well and it's certainly very true of humans. If we don't reinforce the proper behaviors in employees, the behaviors cease to exist.

The average employee, even if motivated internally to achieve something, will be much more highly motivated if we recognize their achievement because that tells them they're on the right path and they'll want to go out and achieve more! It's a self-fulfilling prophecy–our job is to keep the fire within them stoked, not be the ones with a bucket of water.

The big question is: if we know all this, why don't we have a culture of praise and recognition in more workplaces today?

The sad thing is when I ask this question of managers and supervisors, the number one thing I hear is "we don't have enough time." That makes me incredibly sad, how long does it take to say thank you? How long does it take to say, "I appreciate the level of detail you put into those reports"? How long does it take to say, "Thank you for handling that dissatisfied customer so well"?

As leaders, that's our job. Some supervisors are just unaware of the power of verbal praise. Believe it or not, I still speak with people who think "they're getting paid to do their job, so I don't need to thank them."

That may be slightly true, but that doesn't drive engagement.

I've had supervisors tell me, "Why should I recognize someone just for doing their job? I'll recognize them if they do something big."

That's unrealistic. We have many people in the workforce who are steady employees–they're not lighting the world on fire, but they're dedicated, give a full day every day, and we fail to thank them for those efforts. But I'm willing to bet if those people have shortcomings, we're quick to punish them. There needs to be some level of balance with accountability systems–we can't all be negative all the time.

In the next chapter, we'll look at what it takes to give praise appropriately, and in an effective and timely manner. It's time to fix our culture!

"There's no magic formula for great company culture. The key is just to treat your staff how you would like to be treated."

—RICHARD BRANSON, FOUNDER, VIRGIN GROUP

DEVELOPING AN EMPLOYEE-CENTRIC CULTURE

11

Let's assume for a moment that our employees are doing what they're supposed to be doing 95% of the time. This is probably an accurate assessment. But if you think about what you spend your time on as the leader in your organization, I'm willing to bet you spend 95% of your time correcting the 5% of things employees are doing wrong.

The question is: what are we missing here? What's obvious is that we have tremendous opportunity to praise our people but instead, we focus on the few shortcomings they have. We miss out on opportunities to move them closer toward their goals because that last 5% of performance is often the hardest to get. Achievement should become part of the expectation–we want them working hard to master that last 5%.

Ultimately, that motivation results in positive behaviors being exhibited.

When we look at praise in the workplace, it has to be a little more than a pat on the back and a thank you. We must be specific in our praise, not just thanking them for getting the report in on time but perhaps something like, "Thank you for getting that report in on time. It really helped solidify the decisions we needed to make in the executive meeting." It's a little clearer for the employee because we're letting them know why their work was important, and it takes little time!

If we spend more time praising, the results will be a more engaged employee willing to work hard on their own to fix the last 5% of deficiencies. If we focus so much on that 5% we neglect to praise them for the vast majority of things they're doing well, human nature is that they'll say, "Those must be very important so I can let some other things go."

To be clear, I'm not suggesting that we don't correct behavior or that we don't coach and counsel employees. I'm saying we need to keep it in perspective regarding the time and number of things we focus on when it comes to praising versus correcting.

Be Specific!

When we praise, it's critical that we are specific in our praise. I alluded to that above, and I'll give another example here.

I recall several years ago asking an administrative assistant to put together some data into graphic form in PowerPoint for nice visuals for an executive meeting. She did that and really went above and beyond my expectations. The simple graphs I put up on the screen provided a high-level of detail we needed to talk about in the meeting. We were able to come up with a game plan to fix some items we had discussed in the executive session.

WATCH
Is 2% Enough?

I came back to my office and not only said thank you but said, "Your work distilling all that data into a couple of simple charts in which we were able to see patterns was incredibly helpful in us tackling this issue. Thank you for doing that for me."

That was simple, sincere, and individualized praise. The smile on her face was all the payment I really needed! What was even more interesting was when I asked her to do similar things in the future, I got the same type of performance. She knew I not only appreciated her work, but it was exactly what I was looking for. That brief praise had also coached her a little to let her know what was important regarding her performance.

The other thing with praise is it should be proportionate to the level of achievement. For the salesperson who greatly exceeds her goals for the year, I really don't think they should be given little plaque on the wall and a thank you for knocking it out of park this year. That's almost an insult. If that salesperson blew her numbers out of the water, that meant a huge revenue spike for us. Then we thank them with a plaque on the wall?

There are employees who certainly like those things, but they're not proportionate and could be viewed as a slap in the face. We need to recognize that praise and reward must be commensurate with the level of effort it took to obtain the results.

Praise should be frequent and ongoing in workplaces. Too often, the only time praise occurs is for the big things they do. We forget it's the little things employees do well that creates the organization's success on a broader level. If we could look for more opportunities to praise our people, that's more opportunities we have to encourage them and keep them motivated and engaged.

I remember early in my career seeing a spoof on this where a woman was sitting at a sewing machine, charged with hemming a garment. Her supervisor was standing over her micromanaging and throughout the short video clip, her supervisor corrected the seamstress nonstop for five minutes. Literally every step of the way the supervisor found something she was doing incorrectly. It was actually a very painful five minutes to watch and yet, unfortunately, there are leaders out there who believe that's how to manage an employee's performance.

An Encouraging Environment

I believe it's our job to create an encouraging environment, to coach our people through their weaknesses but encourage them through their strengths. My daughter plays golf and is in a struggle with a couple of her shots. For those of you reading who play golf you know it's probably one of the more mental sports out there and if you allow yourself to get mentally frustrated by one part of your game, it flows through into other parts of the game.

My daughter is experiencing that right now. She's finding that the more she focuses on the one part of her game that's not working, the other parts that are her strengths are suffering. So, the other day, rather than going to the driving range working on long irons (her struggle right now), we went out into the backyard and chipped into the chipping net.

Chipping and putting are her strong points. Working on something she's already pretty good at might seem counterintuitive. But in effect, she's laughing and smiling as we're having mini competitions of who can get more balls into the net. It was a fun practice session for her, and that's what she needed. I wanted to break the mental cycle in her that working too much on her weakness was creating.

There is a point in our role as leaders where we must focus on positives. If we go back to the idea that 95% of the time people are doing the right things, let's not forget to focus on those things, praise our people for those things, and thank our people for those things.

Let's be encouraging of them so they continue on! Because here's the thing: the girls my daughter plays golf with are pretty solid in their long game so as a team, they're tough to beat. These two girls have really good tee shots but my daughter is better around the green, so they achieve really good scores in their tournaments.

When you look at your workforce, isn't the same true? The people on your work team have different strengths and it's likely that one person's strengths lie in an area where other employees are struggling. If we build each person up around the 95% of things they do well, we'll have a solidly performing team. That's really all we're tasked with as leaders: to build a high performing team.

How to Praise Effectively

Let's go through specifically how we could tailor praise. Praise should be:

Specific. We must get things like "nice job" and "nice work" out of our vocabulary because those phrases don't mean anything. We must use descriptive language and examples.

When I'm working with my daughter on the golf course, I don't say "nice swing." I read somewhere there are 64 muscles involved in making the golf swing work. That's a lot of moving parts!

So, I'll say, "Wow, you had your hands placed perfectly on the club for that stroke. Your thumbs were in the right position and the clubhead was facing the right direction." That praise is specific, so she knows what to do next time.

After constructive criticism, I'll say, "See what happened when you made that adjustment? Do you see how you were able to control your swing better?"

She looks at me and I see the lightbulb going off in this 11-year old's eyes. Our adult employees think and respond the same way to the specificity in what we're talking about. As I shared earlier in the anecdote about my administrative assistant, the lightbulb went off in her eyes when I thanked her specifically for turning our data into easily understandable graphs. Then she realized, "Ed not only appreciated my work, but it really helped him. I'm going to incorporate that into all the work I do for him!"

Sincere. People sometimes struggle with this, but the next thing praise must be is sincere. If we cannot be sincere in our interactions with our people, I'm not sure we should be in the position of a leader. I realize sometimes, we may not be in the right frame of mind to show sincerity. We have our struggles too as leaders. If you're in a funky state of mind I would simply suggest waiting until your head clears and you can be sincere so you can really connect with your employees while giving them praise.

Good leaders connect with their people. Sincerity comes out when we can show our genuine excitement in their achievements and follow that up with the expression of confidence they can do it again.

Think about the last time you were excited by something someone did. Maybe it was your child or maybe it was an employee. I'm willing to bet your whole demeanor changed–the words you chose, your body language, the tone of your voice all exuded excitement.

You can't force or fake that, and that's why sincerity is so critical to letting our people know our true appreciation for their efforts. We're not just simply saying thanks. Sometimes there are little things we can do for our people, whether it's a small handwritten note or buying them a cup of coffee. The little things along with our words can really convey sincerity.

Individual. We have to individualize our praise. We have to take those words we're speaking with a tone and attitude of sincerity and make them individual to that person.

For example, if that person has struggled with a piece of their performance and is mastering it, we might say something like, "I know you've worked hard to develop this skill set and it's really showing. The results are happening, and I'm thrilled for you."

That praise is specific to them and goes beyond "thanks for your hard work." We've mentioned the specific skill they're working on and that we appreciate the fact they've worked so hard to develop it.

The message here is that it's all about connecting with the individual. Leadership expert John Maxwell actually wrote an entire book on this topic which he called *Everyone Communicates, Few Connect*. It's so true of all of us and today, with all the means of communication we have, we're able to deliver information faster than ever before but perhaps not better than ever before because often we're missing that human connection. That's what's going to drive our people's performance.

We talked about praise being proportionate. It must reflect the extent to which the goal was achieved and the effort it took to get there. Again, you must know your people and know what it is that will motivate them.

The other night after the kids won their golf match, the parents took the kids out and let them get big desserts they could all share. Kids love that! It was fun for them after a hot night on the course working together as a team to win their match.

It can be really simple.

Readers might say, "Gee Ed, that might work for kids" but the simple things make all the difference for our people. It need not be huge, but I also don't believe it's a plaque on the wall. We must know our people.

There's a great book on the topic called *Hug Your People* by Jack Mitchell in which he talks about getting to know the little things about your people. For example, if a lady in the office is celebrating her birthday, don't give her roses if you know she likes daisies! If one of your employees is a dad running his kids around town to soccer and ballet, maybe he'd appreciate a gas card. It's the little things we do for our people that are individualized and proportionate to their achievements and efforts that make a difference.

I was working with a client a few years ago who told me he really put one of his senior managers through the wringer. They were working on a big project and the owner was leaning on this gentleman to bring the project home. And he did! He knocked the project out of the park, landed a new client, and made a lot of money for the company.

The owner knew the gentleman had a well-deserved vacation coming up. Around Friday at lunch, he said, "Why don't you head home now and take an extra half-day for your vacation?" And he handed him a check that covered the cost of the vacation.

That praise was proportionate to the effort this employee put in over six to nine months to not only land the new client but prepare the company to succeed in managing the new client work.

The business owner did this of his own accord, but it was individualized, sincere, and certainly proportionate to the level of effort. The employee told me he had worked at the company for a number of years, almost since its inception, and had never seen the owner do that. He was blown away.

What better reaction do we want from our people?

I don't think employee relations is hard. I actually think it's easy.

If we believe that 95% of the time our employees are doing things right, 95% of our communication with our people should be positive. Experts believe that your praise-to-correction ratio should be 4 to 1 overall through the course of a year. That means that for every time we had to correct someone, we want there to be four other times where we praised the good things they did.

LISTEN
The Leveraging HR Podcast

In my early days at UPS as an operations supervisor, I was expected to review operations reports from the day before to find the three "least best" performers and talk to them about why their performance down. As a young supervisor, I would certainly do what was expected of me as part of the company culture, but what a cruddy way to start the day! Find the three worst performers and talk to them about why they had a crappy day before. Not only was that a cruddy way for me to start the day, but it was also cruddy for them too!

But I was expected to do it, so I decided if I had to talk to the three bottom performers every day, I would talk to the three top performers, too. I found that typically the bottom performers were at the bottom because something crazy had happened on road. They weren't the same bottom or top performers daily.

What my employee group came to understand through this was I would talk to them about the good and the bad. UPS culture at the time was not one where you praised a lot. It was very heavy-handed with needing to "fix the problems."

I just decided that wasn't who I wanted to be as a supervisor. I didn't want to always be seen as "Here comes Ed, that must mean I screwed up." It's not my style or personality. So, my work group understood if I had to talk to them about their poor performance, they would also get praise when they knocked it out of the park.

Our people must understand that. As adults, they expect to be counseled when their performance is down. It's a demotivator when we fail to do the other side and recognize them for doing well.

Finally, praise should be encouraging. When someone has success, we not only need to let them know we appreciate it but that it's something they should expect of themselves once they see they can do it. We should be talking about how they can replicate their performance because we value their performance so much. That comes through an ability to be sincere with a person when praising.

As I mentioned in the story with my administrative assistant, she stepped up her game and I didn't even have to ask her to. Because of the message I gave her, she started doing it repeatedly and I kept praising her. The first couple of times I said, "Gosh, I thought you knocked it out of the park the first time and now you've done it again. This is awesome work!" And I meant it! It was awesome work and it made my life much easier.

She stepped up her game simply because I took the time to praise her appropriately and stress I valued that behavior. Whatever we stress and show we value in our employees is what they will exhibit for us, good and bad.

How we practically apply engaging employees through proper praise and encouragement requires looking through the lens of different relationships present in the office. What do the relationships look like between managers and direct reports? What about peer to peer and between departments? If you have a coaching or mentoring type of culture in your organization, what does that look like between coach or mentor and employee?

We must ask these questions because there are spaces where encouragement and culture can fail if one set of relationships isn't in sync.

We must make praising and encouraging part of our to-do list as managers like I did at UPS when I talked to my best performers daily. As leaders charged with solving problems, it's easy to get caught in the negativity of "all I do is put out fires." Maybe some fires wouldn't start if we made part of our to-do list encouraging people and praising them for jobs well done.

I was working with an organization whose CEO never leaves his office. He doesn't interact with his employees or customers and when he does leave the office to go from one meeting to the next, his head is down.

This sets a tone of toxicity throughout the organization. The rest of the C-suite is not getting the leadership they need, so they're struggling to share the vision with their people. People see the person whose job it is to set the vision not living the vision. We must get out of our comfort zones to do these things with our people. I would even suggest if you're in a larger organization you track the types and amount of praise being delivered to your people. You only need to do this for a short period to see what your front-line leadership is spending their time doing. You might be surprised at how little time they're spending praising people and how little we actually recognize our people.

I was recently in the town next to where I live and had banking to do so I went to the local branch there and was amazed that on the digital screen flashed a photo of a teller at my own branch. She was the employee of the month throughout the institution, not just at the local branch.

I thought that was really cool, and the next time I went to my branch I said, "Hey Sarah, I saw your photo up at the branch the next town over and it was so cool! Congratulations."

She just beamed that I had mentioned that. Obviously, I'm a customer, not her supervisor but it's just part of my DNA. She was recognized as employee of the month and I know I'm always pleased with the service she gives me so why wouldn't I let her know I saw her picture and think it's pretty cool?

If we're going to track the art of praise or lack thereof being delivered, what type of results can we impact if we start to move those praise numbers up? What might we see? What might we be willing to do to get a more engaged workforce? And when we get there, let's celebrate it!

I want to end this chapter with a note of caution: if we work hard to develop a sense of employee engagement and a positive work culture, it doesn't take hard work to lose it. In fact, it's easier to lose that culture than to maintain it.

Once we've instilled the culture we want in our organization, we must work tirelessly to maintain that. Part of that maintaining is not only in praise but in how we fit our teams together.

In the next chapter, we'll look at how we take this employee-centric culture and use it to reward our people for achieving business results.

"If you pick the right people and give them the opportunity to spread their wings and put compensation as a carrier behind it you almost don't have to manage them."

—JACK WELCH, FORMER CEO,
GENERAL ELECTRICVIRGIN GROUP

INCENTING THROUGH VARIABLE PAY

12

Often when I'm speaking with executives, they tell me that one thing that keeps them up at night is how to motivate their people towards high performance and how to keep them performing at peak capacity.

There are a number of different ways to do this, and in this section, I will talk about financial incentives for our people. Often when I talk about financial incentives, invariably I hear from HR "my people aren't motivated by money."

I agree that we all have different motivating factors in why we do what we do, but the reality is we all want to feel valued for our contribution towards our organization. That value comes from a number of different areas, mainly because of how we're treated and the meaningfulness of the work we're doing.

Especially in an economy where our time is valued in dollars, we must be sure we're incenting our people and especially our high performers to attain bottom-line business results for us.

I recall one executive I was speaking to who was a small business owner. He was lamenting that if his top salesperson continued to produce at the rate he was, according to the commission plan in place, that salesperson would out earn the business owner that year.

The business owner was struggling with that and he had asked me to redesign the commission structure to put a cap on the salesperson's earnings.

I eventually talked him out of that for one simple reason: we need to pay our people what they're worth when they are driving business results for us.

This owner was being short-sighted, failing to realize that the success of his business was being driven largely by this person! By disincentivizing this person, his bottom line would ultimately suffer and hence his own paycheck would as well.

I'm a big believer that while we can do many things to incent our people, we want to use different types of variable pay to keep people focused on activities that will drive our business results.

If we build a variable pay plan in our organization, the ultimate goal of that plan must be to improve our organization's performance. There is no other reason to incent people beyond their base pay other than to drive business results.

A well-designed variable pay system will do several things for us.

First, a well-designed variable pay system helps create focus and identify what's important in our organization. What behaviors drive your business performance? This system can also drive alignment and emphasize the balance between our organization's success and our individual employee's success. They see that bridge we talked about in earlier chapters and understand that what they do matters.

Variable pay is an especially great system to use when trying to facilitate change in our organization—when we want to drive different behaviors. I recall designing a program for an organization where they were having difficulty changing the culture to one focused on safety in the workplace. This client had a very young workforce and with that comes the thought that they're invincible. It was a mostly male workforce and it was a physically demanding job, so there was a sense that they didn't have to pay attention to safe practices because they're physically fit, young, and "invincible."

Because of that, one particular shift in this organization was in the bottom five nationwide of all shifts in this company in terms of its safety record. The management team wanted to change the culture. In this case, we didn't use money to facilitate the change–we used food!

Often when folks think about variable pay, they go right to money (and we will certainly focus on that) but there are other things we can use. In this case, food was a big driver. The safety committee decided that if the shift went one week without an injury (which was a stretch at the time), they'd have a big pizza party for the shift.

It didn't happen the first week. It took a couple of weeks for them to go five straight working days without any type of even minor reportable injury. So, we finally bought them pizza and had the party, and they were happy. For this demographic, this was a big motivator for them!

They asked us what was next. We said, "Okay, let's stretch it out and go two weeks. If you can do two weeks, we'll do a big cookout and management will do the cooking. Burgers, dogs, everything."

Two weeks later, we had a big cookout.

I recall one guy yelling, "What are we gonna do next?"

I said, "Do you think you can go a month?"

They're all cheering and hollering, and I said, "Okay, if you can go a month, we'll buy you a steak dinner."

They went a month and we took the whole shift out for a nice steak dinner.

We were several months into this change at that point, so we didn't need to continue to do these things on a daily, weekly, or monthly basis. We continued with some drawings and raffles as incentives within a 6-month period, and this shift went from one of the worst in the country to one of the best and actually the best in their geographic region.

The incentive program helped them focus on what was important, provided positive reinforcement, and helped facilitate that change!

VISIT
Employee Alignment Webpage

Often, when I share that story business owners will say, "Ed, that costs a lot of money!"

But in the big scheme of things, no, it doesn't. When we totaled the spending on worker's compensation costs versus all the incentives, the incentives came to about 20% of the worker's compensation costs. I'll trade that every day, all day long on ROI!

Regardless of the incentive program we use, whatever the financial investment is, it must drive ROI. If the incentive isn't driving ROI, we must stop doing it.

Variable pay can fall into three general buckets:

Incentives. An incentive has criteria determined in advance. Think commission for a salesperson, perhaps a flat percentage of sales. The amount of payment can vary but regardless, that criteria has been determined in advance.

Perhaps the higher their goals are, and the closer folks get to those goals, their commission increases because we're stretching them further. These incentives can be monetary or non-monetary as in the case I just talked about, which was non-monetary, but the criteria were still determined in advance.

The key is that incentives must be self-funded. If our forecasting shows we will spend more on incentive packages than what we'll get in ROI, we must look elsewhere or redefine the criteria because incentives are non-discretionary. Once we tell our people, "If you do this you will get X," we're breaking a good faith contract with our employees if we don't follow through. Once we break that trust, we may never get it back.

Bonuses. Often people interchange bonuses and incentives, but they're actually different. Bonuses are typically associated with completing a task.

For example, I know many organizations that are encouraging of education. Those organizations may give someone a bonus for attaining a master's degree. With bonuses, the amount of the bonus is determined in advance—maybe you receive an extra $1,000 for getting your master's degree.

WATCH
Bonuses vs. Pay Raises

Bonuses are typically monetary, and we have to budget for them. They're also non-discretionary. We're not talking about spot awards here for employees going above and beyond, so you give them a gift card as a quick recognition. Bonuses are about "if you complete this task, you get this reward."

Bonuses differ from incentives in the sense that incentives are typically related to something a little more long-term. For example, a salesperson's commission structure is based on how they perform over the course of a year and incentives are typically paid out during the year, whether that's monthly or quarterly. A bonus, on the other hand, is a one-time payment, such as you finish this book, you get $1,000.

Recognition. The third type of variable pay system falls under the broad category of recognition. These are things we do spontaneously. An employee goes above and beyond for us, maybe we hand them a $10 gift card. It's that sort of thing, where the decision for an award is made after the fact. Bonuses and incentives are laid out in advance as specific rewards, but recognition is not.

Recognition-based rewards are made after the fact, such as an owner or executive sitting there saying, "Sue really went above and beyond so I'll give her a night out with her significant other." The decision is made after the fact and it's still focused on employee behaviors.

We don't want recognition to be just a random act of kindness. We want it to be directly related to something an employee has achieved for us. Recognition could be monetary or non-monetary (like a plaque), but this type of reward is purely discretionary. There are no guarantees for going above and beyond, it truly is spontaneous. Yet, we still must budget for recognition awards.

Recall my earlier story of the owner whose employee had just driven results beyond what the owner could have ever dreamt of? The employee was getting ready to go on a pre-planned, well-deserved vacation with his family (I believe he was going on an international cruise).

The owner gave him a check for the cost of the cruise and said, "Your vacation is on me."

This was purely a spontaneous situation, and it was monetary, but it was purely discretionary. This employee wasn't expecting it or working towards it, which is what makes it recognition based.

Our variable pay system should fall into one of those three buckets for us to have a well-conceived system that drives business results for us.

WATCH
Ghost Hunter

The reason to use variable pay in an organization is that it helps clarify the important tasks employees must perform and the results they must accomplish. Variable pay helps us provide positive reinforcement. That's key, especially where we're crushed under a lot of business coming in.

I talked to an owner the other day who was 300 orders backed up. His business is weather-driven, so in inclement weather he gets even further behind. Some people might think that's a nice problem to have (and it is) but it also requires a focus on his employees to keep them motivated to continue to dig out from behind that kind of a backlog.

Variable pay can also encourage motivation through continuous improvement. It can create a sense of, "I accomplished this, so what if I accomplish even more? Can I get a bigger bonus or up my incentive package?"

But remember to emphasize that balance between the organization's success and business performance. We cannot get into a situation where we're rewarding individuals for their performance while the business as a whole is suffering.

That's why I mentioned earlier that variable pay systems must be self-funding. If the business isn't getting ROI, a bonus or incentive plan simply can't get funded.

One of the biggest decisions to make when putting a variable pay plan into place is how it will be laid out based on an employee's level in the organization.

For example, any variable pay plan for C-level folks must be 100% based on the company's success. If the company isn't successful, there can't be a variable pay payout to the C-level executives. Nearly daily in the headlines we'll see a story about a company whose profits are down and is going bankrupt, yet the top executive gets a multimillion-dollar bonus. That makes zero sense because that bonus should be tied to how well the company is doing, and clearly in those situations, the company is not doing well!

I recall working with a board of directors to establish board governance procedures and assist them in developing a better relationship with their CEO. Through the course of the project, I learned the CEO was upset he had not received a bonus the previous year. Turns out he had a robust list of Key Performance Indicators to hit, and he hit most of them...except the one labeled as the "kill switch." The organization failed to hit its revenue target, thereby negating any opportunity for a bonus. This is a perfect example of a variable pay plan that must be self-funding. It took a long discussion between us for him to see that simply hitting the nonmonetary items wasn't enough. In fact, I challenged him to determine whether hitting some of those KPIs may have caused the company to not hit its revenue goals. The system has to all work together to achieve desired outcomes and reward our people.

Mid-level management is often the rubber band, pulled by the C-level to get business results and pulled by the line staff to get what's in the line staff's best interest. I believe that for middle management, a portion of their variable pay must be based on the company's success, and the other portion must be based on their individual team's success.

To keep the numbers simple, let's say we design a variable pay plan where 50% of the money is determined by the company's success and the other 50% is determined by their team success.

It's possible for a manager to get full, half, or none of their bonus. Here's how:

If the manager's team achieves the desired results and the company has achieved its predetermined results which fund the plan, the manager gets 100% of their bonus

If the company does well but that manager's individual team didn't hit their goals, the manager would get half of the eligible bonus because their team didn't drive success.

What happens if the team is successful, but the company is not? This is a point people love to argue. They'll say, "Ed, they should get a bonus because their team was successful."

It comes back to: where is the money coming from if the company isn't successful? Earlier in the chapter, I said these plans have to be self-funding. If the company had no successful cycle, there's no money in the till to award the incentive plan.

We must keep a stiff upper lip here in communicating to employees that the only way we achieve success is if the company itself is also successful. Ultimately the danger in awarding payouts in these circumstances is creating a "handout" mentality amongst the team.

There are exceptions to every rule and certainly, sometimes, an executive might decide to reward the team despite the revenue numbers being off, but that should be the exception to the rule.

What about bonuses for line staff?

Because they can only control what they're doing and not what the company is doing, individual effort should be weighted higher than company success. For ease of numbers, let's assume that 20% of the incentive plan is based on company success and 80% on individual effort.

The same situation applies to line staff as management. Only if the company succeeds can they get any bonus whatsoever. These percentages aren't hard and fast, we're using them for example purposes only—but what's important to remember is that the balance of those percentages must reflect the culture we're trying to drive in our organization.

The thing that must stay the same for everyone down through the organization is that a percent of the bonus must be relative to the company's success. That's the only way we can get everyone moving in the exact same direction, driving business results and staying focused on those results.

In very broad terms, we can look at short-term incentives and long-term incentives.

We want to choose between short-term or long-term incentives based on the focus we want our people to have. Let's start off with short-term incentives.

Short-term Incentives

One of the most popular short-term incentives is profit sharing, where folks receive rewards based on the financial performance of the company. Generally, this will foster employee identification with the organization's success.

Profit sharing helps us create a common focus amongst all the employees. What's important to note here is there is a predetermined formula for allocating the money, so employees know that if we hit a certain revenue number, a certain percentage of payout will happen.

It shouldn't be complicated! If our formula for calculating profit sharing isn't understood by our people, they won't trust it and they won't buy in. I like to use simple numbers we can go after such as net income, gross revenue, or earnings per share. There are pluses and minuses to each, but our people can track and identify with them easily.

The best time to use profit sharing is when we want to promote a common understanding of the business impact among employees and is best used when the employees have the ability to influence profits.

The key is the final word, profits! The company must show a profit for any money to be paid out. Believe it or not, I was called in to help an organization paying quarterly profit shares to employees although they made no profit for three straight quarters. That sends the wrong message to people.

Profit sharing must be simple, centralized, and easy to communicate. It's important that we have only one or two clear measures that get defined to determine success—we can't make it too complicated or again, people won't buy in.

Another type of short-term incentive is called **performance sharing.** Typically, these plans are defined more in certain non-financial criteria that a team or company wishes to achieve. Often, you see performance sharing plans designed at a department level or lower.

Generally, these plans last only for a very specified period of time, but they still must be self-funded. In looking at the safety incentive I mentioned earlier in this chapter, the cost savings we were reaping from not having to pay as much in worker's compensation was funding the food parties we were having for the people. This is the perfect example of a performance sharing plan that's focused on rewarding safety.

With performance sharing plans, standards of performance must be established and incentives must be totally contingent on those standards. Often, performance sharing is used to bolster safety, quality, production, or some other very specific scenarios like bringing a project in on time and under budget.

Performance sharing plans have a much smaller scope than profit-sharing plans. We use performance sharing plans if we want to have a more balanced approach to measuring organizational improvement, rather than just looking at things in profits and revenues. This too can help increase employee understanding of what's really important to the organization. If we're trying to change the company culture, performance sharing is how to go.

Again, people must be able to influence the overall performance. If we're basing the plan on something they can't individually control and contribute to, it will not work.

Ultimately, we want them to identify that their behaviors are affecting the success and results of the organization.

The final short-term incentives plan is individual performance-based incentives.

With **individual performance-based incentives,** employees' performances are the sole basis for payout. This incentive can still focus employees on non-financial measures–it could be something like getting additional schooling we not only pay for but give a raise or bonus when completed.

A salesperson's commission is another perfect example of an individual performance-based incentive.

The best time to use an incentive plan is if you're trying to reinforce a performance culture. There, you want people to compete with themselves but not necessarily with one another. If you have an effective system for managing by objectives in the organization, individual performance incentives can work very well.

Long Term Incentives

There are two basic types of long-term incentives we can look at.

The first is an **equity-based** system. Here the reward is creating equity interest in the company such as a stock sharing plan. If we're a publicly traded company and want to align employees with our shareholder's interests, this is a great plan to use. It also increases employee retention because we can tie stock awards to longevity with the organization.

For example, a company may reward an employee with 100 shares this year as a bonus for achieving their goals, but those 100 shares might only vest over the next five years. It need not be set up this way, but it usually is. It's best to use a stock equity plan when stock is stable or growing. If the stock is devaluing, that's certainly not an incentive for our people.

An equity-based system can be done in private organizations as well in an employee stock ownership plan. This can be done similarly to a publicly traded company.

The second long-term incentive is **non-equity based.** This incentive plan determination has nothing to do with stock performance or the value of the company. Here, we're looking at focusing people's attention and efforts on specific things over the long haul. Typically, we're looking further than a year.

Think about an organization that may need to be strong in research and development, like a car company.

The design or redesign of a new car takes years. So, a company like this may want to have a long-term performance-related plan for someone working on a project of that length.

Without using stock, we're probably looking at a financial-based incentive to focus people's attention and efforts on that particular project. If the company is private and has no stock plan, they can do this. For a public company that may want to conserve stock, this is also a great option.

Regardless of the incentive plan we select based on our needs, the design considerations are the same. We must figure out how variable our people's performance and our company's performance is. For example, is your business cyclical in nature? If you're a firm that relies on the weather, does the weather deter from your business or help you do business? Think of a landscaping business, which is deterred when it rains but booming when it snows.

What are the variables in our business? Do we peak at a certain time of the year? We have to take that into consideration as we're planning out our payments and calculations for those payments. What's the baseline of performance we expect for payout to occur?

Maybe the company earned a profit, but we didn't hit some baseline levels of performance–perhaps productivity actually went down. Do we want hitting a certain level of performance, regardless of revenue, to be a determining factor? Do we want to consider a maximum payout?

I worked with an organization in the lumber business and, unfortunately, they thrive when hurricane season is really bad. They had strict handcuffs on their salespeople's incentive plans for orders coming in from geographic locations hit by hurricanes because they recognize that through no other fault than Mother Nature, sales go up in those areas. They wanted to make sure they were focusing their salespeople on their performance, not on nature.

We also want to think about what to do with individual performance issues within groups. What if someone didn't contribute to the overall success of the organization? Should they be rewarded and if so, how? This is where allotting percentages I mentioned earlier can come into play.

The final thing to think about is when does the payout occur? For me, it's simple–as soon as possible after the results are achieved because we want our people to tie their achievement of the results and the financial reward together. However, this may not always work so maybe we choose a time of the year when we want to provide payouts–some businesses do this in early summer or during the holidays. I'm okay with whatever works for your business if people recognize that the payout is tied to the results they achieved.

Getting Started

Let's talk about how we get started doing this. You have all the tools, so how do you bring it all together? Before we even start to design our plan, we must think about all the internal and external factors that are going to impact the plan.

We must be prognosticators and work over the next quarter, the next year, etc. depending on how far out the plan will stretch. We must determine what's going on internally with the business and what external pressures we will face. Try to work those factors into your plan and account for them.

We should bring a team together to design this plan. I'm a believer this is a situation where people from all levels with a stake in this should also have a voice in it. We don't want just the executives designing the plan. Let's get feedback from the people affected by the plan, the people who will actually drive the results. Let's get their ideas at least on the things to be measured and what will motivate them.

Once we do that, we can actually design the plan.

WATCH
Staff Compensation Strategies

Designing the Plan

The first thing we must do is determine the plan's objectives. Too often I'll get a call from an owner saying, "I want to put in a profit-sharing plan. How do we do it?"

My response is always, "Wait, why? What's the objective you're trying to achieve?"

That's where we must start. Let's not prescribe the medicine until we actually understand the ailment. Think about what you're trying to achieve through a variable pay system and then decide which system is the best one to use to achieve that goal.

Then, we must define who is eligible to participate in the plan. Is this a companywide situation? Is it a department? Or at the individual level? And what are the performance measures we will rely on?

These need to be easily communicated to our people and they must be achievable, even if they're stretch goals. There's no sense putting a plan in place if we're going to put performance measures so far out that people say, "There's no way I can hit that so I'm not going to bother trying."

We must be smart in the measures we try to go after. This is a situation where less is more–we should have only 2, 3, 4 goals at the absolute most. If we select the right one, all we really need is one.

I once saw a plan with 13 different measures. I had no idea what people were supposed to be focused on because there were way too many measures to keep track of. Keep it simple!

The next piece is determining whether the targets were met, and the payout is triggered. This is where our Finance & Accounting function must help us do forecasting and modeling. If we hit the performance targets we identified, what kind of cost savings or revenues have we generated to fund the plan? We must run various models to determine if our goals were hit or not and how much funding has gone into the plan as a result.

Then, of course, we distribute the earnings on the time schedule we previously identified.

Why Incentive Pay Plans Fail

As the saying goes, no good deed goes unpunished. There are certainly danger zones to incentive pay plans. Following are the key reasons they can fail in an organization:

Unclear or conflicting objectives. Let's say I want to reward you for quality, and I tell you that quality is the most important aspect of our work. But then, I design an incentive plan 100% based on the number of widgets you produce, not the quality. This is a conflicting objective that will cause the plan to fail, and I see this all the time.

Lack of management communication. If management doesn't stay focused on the plan and routinely communicate about the plan, it will fail. I see this way too often, that plans are well communicated and well rolled out but then management is silent for the next year. Marginal communication will damage the results and make all the work we put into the plan for naught.

Insufficient advance modeling of the plan. Something within the plan isn't working—maybe it's not self-funding or we're getting in a ditch where we're paying out more than what results are reaping in for us. This happens if we go hastily into the plan without making sure modeling is done. We want to make sure before we implement the plan that if the maximum payout is achieved by our people, we still achieved our revenue goals to reinvest in the organization and fund the plan.

While throughout this chapter I've used several examples that are monetary related, I want to close by stressing that except for the stock bonuses I talked about, any of these items can be used for non-monetary incentives like food parties (though, of course, something like a food party costs money and has a monetary value attached).

WATCH
Driving Employee Alignment

The most important thing you can do is find out how your people want to be incentivized. Don't make these decisions in a vacuum—let your people tell you what will motivate them!

I opened this chapter sharing that an argument I often hear is "my people aren't motivated by money." I hear this a lot, particularly in not-for-profit organizations, who will often say that people are working for them with a sense of mission. This is often true. But it doesn't mean we can't implement some type of variable pay plan related to the mission of the organization and what the people care about.

Maybe the rewards they want are extra time off or casual dress days. It need not be all about money especially if money is tight for you. It's important that if we're going to attempt to change the culture in the workplace, there has to be something in it for the people who are going to put the effort into changing that culture.

In closing, make sure your plan will truly motivate your people and drive the results you seek. If the modeling doesn't show that either thing will happen, you must conceive a different plan to achieve the results you'd like.

We've looked at our people strategy from nearly every angle. What we have not yet looked at is how well our HR function is performing. In the final chapter, we'll look at how to assess our HR function to determine where we start with overhauling that function.

"The value of a business is a function of how well the financial capital and the intellectual capital are managed by the human capital. You'd better get the human capital part right."

—DAVE BOOKBINDER, AUTHOR, *THE NEW ROI: RETURN ON INDIVIDUALS*

TAKING A STRATEGIC LOOK AT YOUR HR FUNCTION

13

When I think about assessing the HR function of an organization, I believe that the assessment's sole purpose is to review the implementation of our organization's policies and procedures, not simply to ensure compliance with employment laws. We also must look at how we implement best practices and educate our management team.

Any assessment of an HR function that doesn't include those things is not giving us the full picture of how well that function is serving the needs of the business.

Once we undertake this, we then must decide how much of the HR function we want to assess. Do we want to look at everything HR is doing, or do we want to home in on specific areas? For instance, we may simply want to look at compliance or see how well HR complies with its own policies and procedures. We may want to assess HR efficiency or look at how HR is delivering its services to the organization. There are many ways we can look at assessing the HR function to determine its effectiveness in driving business results.

I believe that's the only reason we would undertake such an initiative. Assessing any function in our business is a very time-consuming proposition, but it's one well spent if we're using it to uncover key opportunities for improvement.

I believe that is one of the biggest benefits of assessing our HR function. The assessment will help us determine the contribution HR is making to the rest of the organization. I also think that too often, HR is not viewed as enough of a professional department as compared to perhaps finance and accounting or sales and marketing.

Yet we know HR is responsible for some of the biggest budget line items in the business with people management, so it's important that HR be recognized as a professional function just like any other department in our organization. But one of the most important reasons we look at how well our HR function is performing is so we can find and solve problems smoothly.

We so often, especially in a growing business, forget that we're putting band-aids on problems and sooner or later, they will not be enough to hold things together. Taking a deep breath and stepping outside is a great way to look at whether any department, not just HR, is serving the current needs of the business.

At a recent conference, I talked about the concept of employment branding–specifically how that impacts a business's ability to recruit and retain talent in a tough labor market. Immediately following that session, a CEO came up to me, handed me his card, and said, "Ed, we've gotta talk."

The following week, we discussed the fact that his organization was growing so fast that HR could not keep up with the growth. He said, "We keep adding people to the HR function and it's not making a difference."

My response to that statement was, "That's part of your problem." Throwing people at the situation without understanding why we have the problem in the first place will not lead to a solution.

He said, "I completely agree," and we worked together to look at what was going on inside the HR function. This was a holistic assessment. Because I was able to come in from the outside with unbiased views, I was able to quickly see a number of things folks very close to the situation couldn't see. There were no procedures in place for very common things HR was doing, which was evidenced by the fact that multiple people in HR had their hands in certain processes and were doing pieces of processes, but no one owned the whole process. There were tons of inefficiency.

I wasn't convinced they had the right people doing the right jobs in HR, so we instituted some changes in roles. We also uncovered that one recruiter wasn't effective at recruiting and found her a new role that was a match for her skill set.

This is just a small taste of what we uncovered, to illustrate that if we have no grasp of what's going on inside HR in processes and procedures, the larger our organization gets, the more we expose ourselves to inefficiencies that are going to hold back the organization.

As of the time I stepped in to look at the HR function, this business had just shy of 800 employees. There were 35 openings and they were building another facility across town to generate another 40 openings. HR was already behind in its recruiting and the number of open positions would double in the next 4 months. It was a recipe for disaster for any organization.

Again, it wasn't that HR wasn't attempting to do its job. But it had no strategic direction, very few documented processes, and many folks in HR were doing pieces of various processes leading to all of this inefficiency holding this organization's growth back.

If we're going to do an assessment, we must decide what kind of tools we want to use. There are four things we can do based on the assessments we want to do. I'll list the tools here:

Interviews. This is a time-consuming piece of the process but it's absolutely critical. Sitting down with the key stakeholders, whether they be inside HR or outside the HR function, is important. We must assess what the folks in various HR roles are doing and what they perceive the challenges to be, as well as sit down with those affected by HR, including department managers, the C-suite, and ownership.

Another organization I worked with is a professional services organization with 20 different partners who are all owners of the organization. In assessing their HR function, I sat down with several members of their ownership team. It was important to get their views on how HR was or was not supporting them.

The C-suite was also important to sit down with. Those folks were hired by the partners to run the business so the partners could focus on their areas of expertise. It was important to get their perspective on how HR was serving them and where their challenges were.

Interviewing takes a lot of time, but I always start there because it's probably the most effective method we have of uncovering challenges.

Document review. This isn't the most exciting part of the process, but it is necessary. The documents I like to review are the documented processes within the function. What are the standard operating procedures we have outlined? Are they serving the organization or not, based on the information I uncovered during the interviews?

This is a great opportunity to determine whether our processes are outdated and no longer serve us. It's also a great opportunity to identify where we don't have processes in place- because when we don't have processes in place, we find that employees just "wing it."

Questionnaires. In extremely large organizations, one way to shave time off an assessment is through questionnaires. I handled an extremely large organization's audit of its pay practices and because they had several thousand employees spread out over several states, we used that approach.

It was an anonymous survey where employees were asked to provide feedback on pay and benefits—that was the scope of this particular assessment. These assessments may not give us the level of detail an interview would but with time and geographic constraints, we can amass a lot of data quickly and efficiently to give us the direction we need to go especially with our document review.

Data sampling. This is the final tool we can use.Occasionally, I like to ask for pockets of data such as 10% of the resumes of people an organization didn't hire or the files of the last twenty people who left the organization. From there, we can see if there are trends happening.

Again, this is a time-consuming step but based on the desired outcome of the assessment it may be an important one. I often hold this one for last, especially if I'm hearing disconnects in what I've uncovered in interviews versus what I'm seeing as documented procedures or processes. Then, I like to sample to get a better idea of what's really happening in the organization.

Those four tools can be used in any combination to give us the data we need to make an assessment on the efficiency of our HR function.

What to do with the data collected?

There are a few different ways to use the data. The first would be to assess what I like to call managerial compliance. In other words, are we following our own personnel policies, procedures, and legal provisions?

I recently served as an expert witness in federal court where the entire case centered on whether or not the company had received several legal documents from the plaintiff. The company had alleged that it hadn't received the documents and was requesting additional time to review those documents to defend its case.

When the vice president of HR took the stand, the judge lambasted him because there were numerous deficiencies in the way this organization administered its process for handling any legal communications coming into the organization.

In this VP's defense, this situation happened before he arrived at the company. However, under direct questioning from the judge he was forced to admit that even when he found out about the proceedings, he didn't investigate to see why the information didn't make it to his legal counsel's desk. There was no written procedure for handling these types of things and he didn't even know who was at the front desk on numerous occasions.

I tell this story to illustrate this company is facing a half a million-dollar lawsuit largely because it had no process in place and employees educated on that process of what to do when legal documents arrived at the corporate offices.

This may be an extreme example, but it shows us that failing to have processes we follow can have devastating consequences. I often like to go into an organization and ask them for their processes. Then, I ask them to show me how they're complying with their own processes.

Just because they're not complying with their own processes doesn't mean they're inefficient. Perhaps the process needs to be redone. If there is a process in place, we must see why it's being short-cut and whether the shortcuts are okay to continue–in which case, we update the process. Alternatively, do we need to create a process or educate people on the existing process and get back to doing things the way we have them documented?

The next thing to look at in an assessment of HR is the climate or culture of the organization: the impact that the organization is having on employee motivation, morale, and job satisfaction.

If we decide this is what we want to measure, we must look at things like employee turnover, absenteeism rates, safety records, and maybe employee opinion survey results. We may also want to conduct focus groups with employees.

These things will tell us how well HR is serving the needs of its employees. With the assessment of managerial compliance, we're looking at how well HR is serving the needs of the business. With climate, we're looking at how well HR is serving the needs of its employees. An HR function must do both effectively to be an effective function.

I recall an organization that asked me to run focus groups for them because for several straight years, their employee opinion survey results were declining. They had even conducted a best places to work survey for the past few years and those results were declining as well.

We decided that rather than doing any individual interviews, we would run the focus groups and fill them with cross-sections of people from the union folks in the warehouse to IT to accounting to sales. But there was no one from HR or management in the focus groups. We made that decision so employees would feel they could be open with me.

Those focus groups identified several key areas for management to address the surrounding decline in employee opinion surveys. One of the biggest things we uncovered was a lack of communication. Employees didn't feel they had enough information about things going on in the company including why their medical benefits were changing year after year.

This lack of communication was affecting morale and productivity. We helped HR craft new messaging that was more frequent, less wordy, and directed to the needs of specific work groups.

From that shift, we saw morale change. People didn't feel like they were in the dark anymore.

Once we decide which type of assessment we want to do, whether it's managerial compliance or our HR climate, we must think about our approach.

There are 5 different approaches we could take, and none are better than any other. Sometimes a mix and match approach, based on what situation is presented with any particular organization, is appropriate. I simply select the approach based on what I believe fits the situation at hand.

The Comparative Approach

The first approach I use is a comparative approach where I sit down with company leadership and ask them to give me the names of some organizations they admire. They may be in a different geographic area, within or outside of the industry, perhaps they're competitors.

Once I have that, I do research on those organizations. If I can get information such as their employee satisfaction rates, turnover, wages, and benefits, we can then use that to compare to our organization.

You can think of this as a model company. Maybe they're the gold standard in your industry and you're striving to be like them. Getting hold of key data points from their organization may tell you how far from being a model company you are.

There are a lot of pros and cons to each approach that I'll outline here. Some pros to this approach are that if you can garner this information from the model company and work to fill those gaps, you may attract the same high-level talent they're attracting.

The cons are that it's difficult to get this data. Usually, the model company isn't going to just open their books and tell you all their secrets.

The other con with this approach is that every organization is unique. Similar to being unable to compare yourself to another person with their different circumstances and talents, no organization (even in the same geographic area and industry) will be exactly like you. You'll need to take the results they're getting and adapt it to your organization.

But if you can get the data you want, the comparative approach is a great approach.

Outside Authority

The next approach is often called the outside authority approach. This one deals with assessing your HR function against a set of benchmarks established by some outside criteria.

Think about an organization that may be going through an ISO certification. They are meeting standards set by an outside entity to certify that they have a high level of quality in the processes in their organization.

The pros of this approach include seeing the gold standard when it comes to benchmarking and how we compare against it. This can be a humbling exercise because we're likely to fall short in many areas.

The cons are that we're comparing ourselves against the gold standard. It's the same as the pro. What I mean by that is there may be unrealistic expectations or items that don't necessarily translate well to your business in those benchmarks.

That's not a reason to not explore benchmarking against the gold standard, but we must be able to take those results and distill what they mean for us and our organization.

Statistical Measures

The next approach is to stay purely internal and just look at statistics. By this I mean we look at statistical measures of performance we want to be at and compare to where we currently are. For instance, I had a client tell me they were proud of the fact that they had a 5% turnover compared to the industry average of 8%. Sounds good, right?

My response to them was, "So what? Your closest competitor is 100 miles away. Comparing that percent to yours means nothing."

What means more is who is in the 5% that's leaving your organization? The statistical approach is not just about comparing numbers for number's sake but digging into what's behind the numbers. Why do we have 5% turnover? Who are the ones leaving? Is the bulk of that 5% leaving our top performers? That's a serious problem. Is the bulk of that 5% our worst performers? Great, hold the door open for them! We must understand what's behind the percentage and not just pat ourselves on the back that the number is what it is.

Another client was happy to report they were leading the market with pay. That sounds good on the surface. They were almost 20% ahead of the market, so one would think the employees were happy because they were the highest paid in the industry.

The employees were happy, honestly! The organization had next to no turnover and folks were relatively productive. But the organization was slowly putting themselves out of business because their operating costs were 20% higher than their competitors. They were so proud of that percentage that they weren't looking at what that number was doing to their business.

The pro to this approach is that if we can get the story behind the numbers, we've got some really good data to play with. However, if we just simply stop at a number, we're certainly not getting to the root causes of either our successes or our failures and we're deciding without all the facts.

Compliance

The next approach is the pure compliance approach. In this approach, you'll look at the past actions of the organization to determine if those activities comply with the company's own processes and legal requirements.

For instance, an organization that is a federal contractor would be required to have an affirmative action plan. You could look to see if they compiled an affirmative action plan year after year and if it had all the components to meet the federal requirements.

The pro to the purely compliance approach is we can uncover some traps we might fall into regarding how we're managing our HR function and whether or not we're opening ourselves up to legal actions or fines by the federal government. But the cons to this approach far outweigh the pros. If all we do is look at compliance, we're missing the boat about where HR really contributes to the bottom line.

READ
Audits & Assessments

To be clear, I'm not saying we need not worry about compliance. But if the only thing we ever assess inside of HR is compliance related, we're missing out on high ticket items that truly affect the business performance.

That's why I'm always hesitant to simply do a compliance check. For me, I would rather see that incorporated into a larger scoped assessment than just be the sole thing we're looking at. Our time is better spent on bigger picture items.

Managing by Objectives

Finally, we have the good old managing by objectives approach.

This is where we simply look at the goals the organization or HR function has set for itself and compare those goals against actual performance measures.

I know one client every year audits its effectiveness based on the timeliness of its managers completing all their staff performance reviews. This is an important thing to assess. Performance reviews are often tied to merit increases, and we certainly don't want to be where we're not rewarding people for having a successful year. We don't want them wondering why they put in the effort they did when they're not getting any feedback.

The even darker side of this is to think about the fact that often people contributing to their 401k miss out on any market gains that any additional 401k contributions tied to that merit increase would have garnered for them. By delaying someone's performance review and thereby delaying a raise (even if the raise is retroactive and even if the 401k is retroactive), they still miss out on market gains from the time that money should have been put into their 401k from the time it actually was. In essence, we have punished our people.

This approach is all about setting objectives and measuring performance against those objectives.

One of the pros of this approach is that if we have proper objectives and believe they will lead to business results, it would be very important for us to manage against those objectives and to assess ourselves periodically on how well we're meeting those objectives.

On the flip side, a con is that businesses change. Maybe when we set the objectives we did, we set them with different results in mind or perhaps something has changed in the business, but we never went back and adjusted the objectives. If we're going to assess our objectives, we must make sure they're living, breathing, and current. If they are, then by meeting them we're helping the business achieve the results it desires.

What to focus on?

When we look at the tools we can use, the approaches we can take, and the assessments we can do that will determine how we actually conduct the assessment. That will dictate how we design the questions we will ask based on those criteria.

There are 8 primary components we must focus on within the HR function regardless which of approaches or tools we decide to use.

Those 8 areas are: roles, headcount, and the HR system; recruitment; documentation; training, development and career management; compensation and benefits; performance measurement and evaluation; termination and transition; all things legal.

If we decide we're looking at the entire HR function, those are the 8 things we must look at. We might decide to only look at a piece of the function, and if so, it should be one of those pieces. Everything HR does falls into one of these areas.

As we make the decisions around assessing our HR function, it's not necessarily a linear approach. We might decide which of the primary areas we want to look at and then determine the approach and tools we'll use. We might decide we want to use a different approach or different tools for each of these areas. There is no right or wrong way to conduct an assessment. The only truth is that the items you use must get you the results you desire–those results being the information you need to change your HR function for the better.

Ultimately, if you undertake this, you'll want to document the decisions you've made and all of the results that have come out. Have a formal report to submit to the executive team with the items you've uncovered, or maybe just a binder with this data in it so you can work against the results to improve them.

But if you take the time to assess the HR function, you want to make sure you've documented it, especially including where you've uncovered things of legal or compliance concern that need to be fixed quickly. You'll want to show your due diligence in handling that situation.

WATCH
Strategic HR Audits

Above all else, if you're going to invest time and resources into assessing the HR function, you must be committed to doing something about the results. You could be putting your organization in a much worse situation by uncovering problems and not fixing them than by being ignorant of the problems, to begin with.

In the event of some sort of adverse legal action against us, it will come to light that we knew about these deficiencies. It's important when we head into the process that we're not only willing to commit the time and resources to go through the process, but more important that we're willing to commit the time and resources to fixing what we've uncovered.

CONCLUSION

As we wind down our journey, I think it's always important for us to reflect on what got us here. We started off talking about the current state of HR in the business world—how HR often is inadequate in meeting an organization's needs, irrelevant in the marketplace and often devalued by the executives in their organizations. As we've seen throughout this book, there is a solution to making HR relevant again, and we've captured those secrets inside these pages.

The real challenge that lies ahead is not simply using this book as a guide or checklist, thinking that if you do one thing the relevance and respect will come to your HR function. What I'm really hoping you've heard in this book is that it takes not only a sustained effort to implement and maintain the things we've talked about but it has to be done by someone willing to accept a leadership role in their organization. The leadership role does not require someone to have a "title" attached to it. We can all be leaders.

WATCH
The Bermuda Triangle of Business

But for the HR function to gain the relevance it desires, and today's business environment requires, we must get out of the mode of only thinking about HR in terms of compliance, recruiting, and basic employee relations like party planning. Those three items, while they have some level of value to today's business, do not generate revenue in today's marketplace. No employee or candidate will come knocking on your door because you're in full compliance with labor laws. No one stays with you simply because you have a killer year-end party. It takes the concepts we've discussed inside these pages to have a great employment brand that will attract the best and brightest, keep them motivated while with you, and retain them for longer periods of time.

We have to start with a strategy for our HR function. It all begins there.

As business leaders, we must ask ourselves what we want and desperately need from HR. That must be followed up with implementing training programs that give our people the tools they must be successful and productive for us and drive our business results. As they drive business results for us, more opportunities open for us as business leaders to expand our marketplace and give more opportunities for growth for our people.

The younger generations of today's workforce, millennials and Gen-Z, are no longer asking for opportunities for advancement. They're demanding it of their employers. While they recognize they must get the right skill sets to attain those opportunities, our role isn't just in giving them the skill sets, it's also in providing them with opportunities to use them and grow.

The younger workforce, which in many organizations represents over 50% of employees, also expects and demands an environment of respect and teamwork. We've talked about the path you must follow to build a sense of teamwork and a true team-based culture in the organization. This isn't just for feel-good purposes, but to drive bottom line results.

Finally, we talked about how to incent our people. I believe that more effort is spent on trying to figure out what it will take to motivate people than any other piece of the employment process right now. I don't understand that because I find the solution simple: ask them what they want and do your best to deliver on the things today's employees want and value out of their employment relationship. Maybe it comes back to money, maybe it's about recognition, camaraderie, casual days, or something else. Sometimes it's those simple things that separate us from our competition when it comes to the fight for talent.

This charge must be led by leaders in the organization. Though the concepts I've presented here typically fall under the realm of HR, most can be implemented by anyone in the organization who's savvy enough to understand the importance of a good employment brand. Ultimately, these items must be championed by leaders in an organization—both by leaders in title and leaders that are simply the respected peers inside the organization.

Remember that the path to an excellent employment brand has no final destination. It takes hard work to establish the brand and even harder work to maintain it. It's like anything else we build. If we don't maintain it, it rots and falls apart. Failing to nurture the employment brand we've developed with the action steps in this book will result in falling back into old ways and wondering what happened.

I strongly suggest you not look at this book as a step-by-step process but to think about where your organization is regarding its culture. Then, decide which of the elements we've discussed are the most important to work on right now. While a lot of that must start with having an HR strategy, you may find you need to start elsewhere and that's perfectly okay.

If we don't change how we approach the employment relationship, we will continue to fall behind as business leaders. We won't be able to keep up with our competition and that will ultimately impact the bottom line. If you've heard a common theme throughout this book, it's just that: the only successful path to a robust bottom line runs through our people.

And please note the word *through* our people. Not run over them, run through them. *They* drive the bottom line.

I promise you if you're willing to put the investment, time, effort, and yes, dollars into the processes we've talked about, you will see a return on investment many times over your initial output.

DOWNLOAD
Cultural Readiness Assessment

In closing, they say life is a journey and not a destination. It's my belief the same is true of business success. Success is a journey of constantly reinventing and reevaluating our business model and one in which only the strong survive. Please seize this opportunity to truly reevaluate and reassess where your business currently is and what it will it take to get you back on the path to success (or if you believe you're already on the path, to accelerate the results of that path). I promise you, you'll find that path runs through your people. After all, without good people, we can't provide quality goods and services. No quality goods and services, no customers. No customers, no business. It's a simple equation really. And that's what Bottom Line HR is really all about.

ABOUT THE AUTHOR

Ed works with executives and business owners who are struggling with people problems, such as adapting to changing business conditions and customer, investor, or community expectations.

He turns irrelevant and ineffective HR functions into strategic contributors by aligning HR with the business objectives. As a result, Human Resources actually drives business results.

Prior to entering consulting, Ed spent 12 years with UPS in a variety of Operations and Human Resources management positions. His clients include Fortune 1000 brands Johnson & Johnson, Pfizer, Dana Corporation, Patterson, Dentsply, and Carpenter Technologies as well as Goodwill Industries, Penn State University, the U.S. Army Corps of Engineers, Bosch, and Utz Snack Foods. To date, Ed has completed over 700 projects for more than 250 clients across nearly all industries.

Ed is an advocate for using Organizational Development strategies to drive business results. He speaks to senior leaders across the United States and Canada about how to turn their people into strategic contributors. His audiences include such varied organizations as American Association of Orthopaedic Executives, National Association of Housing Resource Officers, Society for Human Resources Management, CPHR Saskatchewan, New Jersey Banker's Association, and Regional Care Providers Association.

He holds designations as a Senior Professional in Human Resources from the HR Certification Institute; Certified Compensation Professional from WorldatWork;

and SHRM-Senior Certified Professional from the Society for HR Management. He is certified as a speaker, trainer, and coach through The John Maxwell Team, maintains membership in the National Speakers Association, and is a regular contributor to Forbes.com.

When he's not working with clients, Ed can be found teaching at Millersville University. In his free time, Ed relishes spending time with his wife, Heather, and three daughters, Amanda, Emily, and Lea. He enjoys travel, golf, the outdoors, and Notre Dame and Baltimore Ravens football.

Follow Ed on social media

LinkedIn
www.linkedin.com/in/edkrow

Twitter
twitter.com/EdKrowHR

YouTube
https://bit.ly/36OAAML

Facebook
www.facebook.com/edkrowllc

Blog
edkrow.com/blog

Acknowledgements

So many people had a hand in bringing this book to fruition:

The folks at Enlightened Marketing: especially Samantha Hartley who pushed me to envision the possibilities and doesn't take excuses; and Eryn Johnson my amazing Scribe who is a whiz with words. Without all of you I could have never climbed this mountain.

My copy editor, Susan Harbin, thanks to your eagle eyes this book reads better than I could have imagined!

Lay out guru Anthony Smyrski, your creativity shines through and makes this book easy on the eyes.

The team at Yurchak Printing, thanks especially to John W. for your guidance on everything that comes AFTER the writing is complete!

The crew at EZ Solution, especially Tom Malesic and Karri Gonzalez, your insight in navigating social media and the online marketing world has proven invaluable.

The attorneys at Gibbel, Kraybill & Hess, especially Peter Kraybill and Jeff Worley for helping steer me through the copyright process.

My friend and photographer, Rick Titus of Titus Touch Photography, thanks for capturing a great shot of me for the bio page.

And to all the CEOs who shared their stories with me, here's to a better future for HR in your organizations.